Challenging the Traditional Axioms

Benjamins Translation Library

The Benjamins Translation Library aims to stimulate research and training in translation and interpreting studies. The Library provides a forum for a variety of approaches (which may sometimes be conflicting) in a socio-cultural, historical, theoretical, applied and pedagogical context. The Library includes scholarly works, reference works, post-graduate text books and readers in the English language.

EST Subseries

The European Society for Translation Studies (EST) Subseries is a publication channel within the Library to optimize EST's function as a forum for the translation and interpreting research community. It promotes new trends in research, gives more visibility to young scholars' work, publicizes new research methods, makes available documents from EST, and reissues classical works in translation studies which do not exist in English or which are now out of print.

Volume 62 [EST Subseries 3]

Challenging the Traditional Axioms: Translation into a non-mother tongue
by Nike K. Pokorn

Challenging the Traditional Axioms

Translation into a non-mother tongue

Nike K. Pokorn

University of Ljubljana

John Benjamins Publishing Company

Amsterdam / Philadelphia

TM The paper used in this publication meets the minimum requirements
of American National Standard for Information Sciences – Permanence
of Paper for Printed Library Materials, ANSI z39.48-1984.

Library of Congress Cataloging-in-Publication Data

Nike K. Pokorn
   Challenging the Traditional Axioms : Translation into a non-mother
      tongue / Nike K. Pokorn.
      p.   cm. (Benjamins Translation Library, ISSN 0929–7316 ; v. 62)
   Includes bibliographical references and indexes.
      1. Translating and interpreting. I. Title. II. Series.

   P306.P646 2005
418'.02--dc22   2005042120
ISBN 90 272 1668 1 (Eur.) / 1 58811 634 4 (US) (Hb; alk. paper)

John Benjamins Publishing Co. · P.O. Box 36224 · 1020 ME Amsterdam · The Netherlands
John Benjamins North America · P.O. Box 27519 · Philadelphia PA 19118-0519 · USA

Table of contents

Acknowledgements

I would like to thank those who distributed the questionnaire and graciously contributed their time and intuitions to this study: in particular, Prof. Andrew Louth from the University of Durham, Dr. Donal McLaughlin from Heriot-Watt University, Prof. Tom Priestly from the University of Alberta, Prof. Marc Greenberg from the University of Kansas and Prof. Tom Ložar from Vanier College. I am also very grateful to Dr. David Limon not only for his meticulous linguistic revision but also for his invaluable advice and encouragement; and above all, I would like to thank my family, Marko, Žiga and Ivan, for their continuous support and assistance.

Nike K. Pokorn

Introduction

A questioning approach to Translation Studies

Translation into a non-mother tongue or inverse translation, especially of literary texts, has always been frowned upon within Translation Studies in Western cultures with a dominant language, and regarded as an action doomed to failure by both literary scholars and linguists. But despite this traditional "prohibition", literary translation from "minor" into "major" languages has always been carried out by local translators, often working in a pair with a stylistic advisor for the target language. Since this particular translation practice has been more or less ignored by Western translation theory, an attempt is made here to approach it theoretically in order to identify the characteristics and distinguishing features of translations into a non-mother tongue, and to determine the advantages or disadvantages of translators who are native speakers of the target language compared to non-native translators. The study will thus try to find answers to the following questions: Can the native language of the translator be considered as a criterion for assessing the acceptability or even the quality of the translation? Are translations out of one's mother tongue indeed inferior in quality compared to those carried out by native speakers of the TL? On the other hand, do all translators who are native speakers of a major or central linguistic community reveal in their translations from minor languages a limited knowledge of the SL culture and language? Can we identify typical features of the translation that are the result of the translator's or translators' mother tongue?

First, some basic concepts referred to in the study needed to be clarified. Thus Chapter 1 focuses on the commonly-accepted definitions of the terms "mother tongue" and "native speaker". It is established that these two terms are vague, subjective and often defined according to the needs and wants of the individual providing the definition. Bearing this in mind, broad definitions of these terms are adopted for the purpose of the study.

Throughout the text, an attempt is made to remain alert and not to accept in an uncritical way what is already in place, anything that is undertheorised and taken for granted – notions we seem to know so well and which have grown all too familiar to us. Being aware of the perils of ethnocentric and phallogocentric formulations, a mode of thought is nurtured that is essentially non-fixed, unstable and non-rule based, constantly questioning. This stance may seem anarchic at first sight, but the aim is not to disrupt all classifications and definitions or to wallow in indecision: it is rather founded in a desire to express fundamental criticism of the existing power-based order of translation theory. Indeed, I am deeply convinced that Translation Studies needs a questioning approach, revealing "the invisible sclerosis of theory, often not bearing an obvious mark of ideology but, however, systematically strengthening a new form of barbarity coupled with power" (Gorazd Kocijančič 2004: 58). While Translation Studies should remain essentially open to different ideas and also to the possibility of different understandings of the phenomenon of translation itself – from, for example, a hermeneutical, deconstructivist, culturally materialist, post-colonialist or feminist angle – it should also be wary of those manifestations of these categories that fail to recognise their own relativity and try to create an image of objectivity and universality.

In accordance with this position, in Chapter 2 it is established that little actual research has been carried out in Translation Studies concerning the differences between translation into and away from the translator's mother tongue. However, a close reading of some of the fundamental theoretical works reveals that almost all translation scholars have expressed their views on this issue. Although explicit discussions of this problem are rare and frequently restricted to two or three paragraphs, a hidden discourse on translation into a non-mother tongue can often be detected in the discussion of other translational issues, or in definitions of basic terms and concepts. The most widely spread opinion is the "traditional view", according to which translators should translate only into their mother tongue in order to create linguistically and culturally-acceptable translations. I shall argue that this "traditional view" stems from an aprioristic conviction unsupported by any scientific proof that translation into a mother tongue is *ipso facto* superior to translation into a non-mother tongue. Moreover, our discussion reveals that this generally-accepted truth is not, in fact, traditional or universally accepted in either translation practice or theory.

Chapter 3 presents the method used and the corpus for analysis, while the following three chapters focus on an analysis of a selection of texts translated from Slovene into English. The texts chosen for the analysis were originally written in Slovene, a Slavonic language spoken by approximately 2 million speakers in and around the Republic of Slovenia. Slovene was chosen because it is a typical representative of a minor language or "a language of limited diffusion", whose users have always been forced to translate into foreign languages. Translations into a non-mother tongue thus reflect the common practice of minor-language communities. The analysis is applied to literary works, in particular to prose works by Ivan Cankar, the most praised and canonised author in Slovenia, that have been translated into English more than once. The choice of literary works was deliberate: it allowed us to create a corpus of translations where the same text is translated into the same TL by different translators – non-literary texts, on the other hand, only rarely get retranslated. The choice of literary texts may seem to impose certain limitations on this study; however, following the post-structuralist claim that the traditional boundaries between fictional and non-fictional discourse are blurred, and the argument of some literary theoreticians that "literature" is a functional term and not an ontological one (see Eagleton 1983), and that features traditionally applied to literature can be found in non-literary texts and vice-versa, our findings can be interpreted as valid not only for the texts that traditionally belong to literature but to texts in general.

The translators of the selected corpus ranged from native speakers of English or Slovene, through non-native speakers of English or Slovene, to pairs of translators consisting of native speakers of Slovene and English or some other language. Since English is taught at school in Slovenia but does not have the status of the second language, all native Slovene translators had English as a foreign language. The analysis of the texts, following the methodology suggested by van Doorslaer (1995), where Slovene originals were compared to their English translations, shows that none of the commonly-accepted assumptions proved absolutely valid. The translators who were members of a major linguistic community did not necessarily reveal unsatisfactory knowledge of the peripheral source language and its culture. On the other hand, some translators who were native speakers of English revealed scant knowledge of the source language, but at the same time also a questionable competence in English. Then again, some non-native speakers of Slovene or of English showed no lack of understanding of the original or had difficulty in phrasing the target text. The translations carried out by native speakers of Slovene were not necessarily full of improbable collocations and strange turns of phrase. At the same time, surprisingly, the comparison often revealed that even Slovene translators at times failed to understand the source text.

These findings are then compared with another study, involving native speakers of the TL and their response to the selection of previously-analysed translations. The purpose of this second study is to see if the lack of any formal connection between the nationality of the translator and the direction of translation revealed by the textual analysis is also reflected in the response of competent native speakers. A questionnaire was designed for this purpose, which included seven fragments of different English translations of two of Cankar's short stories and a novel. It was answered by 46 competent English native speakers, and it corroborated the findings of the textual analysis. It showed that native speakers were unable to *unmistakably* determine whether the text had been translated by a native or a non-native speaker of English, especially when two translators worked together. It seems that translating in pairs also did not affect the fluency of expression: on the contrary, in spite of the fact that the vast majority of the subjects interviewed chose target-oriented translations as the most acceptable, a translation by a pair of translators was selected as the "best" according to their tastes.

In conclusion, it is observed that translations into a non-mother tongue do not inevitably sound strange to native speakers of the target language; furthermore, translators who are members of major linguistic communities do not necessarily reveal unsatisfactory knowledge of the minor source language and its culture. The study also shows that the status of native speaker does not guarantee that a translator is also a competent user of his/her mother tongue. None of the "traditional" and commonly-accepted assumptions thus proved to be true – the translator's mother tongue proved not to be a criterion according to which the quality of the translation or faithfulness to the original could be assessed. It is therefore also impossible to claim that native speakers of the target language are necessarily more suitable translators than native speakers of the source language or pairs of translators. The study thus concludes that the quality of the translation, its fluency and acceptability in the target language environment depend primarily on the yet undetermined individual abilities of a particular translator, on his/her translation strategy, on his/her knowledge of the source and target cultures, and not on his/her mother tongue and the direction into which he/she is translating.

Open definitions of the terms "native speaker" and "mother tongue"

In order to approach the topic of translation into a non-mother tongue, it is first necessary to clarify the concepts of "mother tongue" and "native speaker", which are fundamental to such a discussion. At first sight, the concepts seem clear enough and sufficiently well-defined; however, a closer examination shows that their definitions are far from objective and water-tight. In fact, the linguistic competence and proficiency of the native speaker are hard, perhaps even impossible to define objectively. And although we all feel that we know who the native speakers and foreign speakers of a particular language are, and that it is not hard to tell them apart, it soon becomes obvious that neither linguistics nor real life provides us with a rigorous and conclusive test which would help us establish a clear distinction between them. Moreover, in some cases, although rare, foreign speakers come close to the group of native speakers of a particular language.

Since the meaning of the concepts of "mother tongue" and "native speaker" seem so unproblematic, it is not surprising then that numerous translation theorists and linguists take them for granted and use them as if their "definitions" had no gaps, no blurred and fuzzy edges. However, despite their pivotal position in both Translation Studies and linguistics, there is considerable variation in the connotations attributed to those terms, which seem to depend on the ideological position of the person providing the definition, or at least on the motives hidden behind his/her need to determine them.

Native speakers of the languages that are regarded as major or core because of the global distribution of power and wealth tend to safeguard their authority and prestige, and therefore rarely grant the status of native speakership to those who were not born into a language but who learned it later in life. When dealing with translations into English from minor or peripheral languages,[1] which are quite often carried out by immigrants, who were not born into the TL culture but who have, however, spent most of their lives within it, the question arises as to whether these individuals should be considered native speakers of the new linguistic community or not.

The concept of "mother tongue"

There are differences in referential meaning and connotation attributed to the concept of "mother tongue". For example, the term can be simply understood literally to denote the language of one's mother, used in her everyday communication with her child. The term is based on the assumption that the child's first significant other is its mother. And indeed, in most cases it is the mother, biological or not, who provides most of the spoken input for the child, and therefore it is with her that the child wishes to exchange meanings. This definition becomes problematic when the child's carer is not its mother but its father, grandparents, foster parents or, indeed, a nanny who is not related to the child. In this sense, the child can have more than one mother tongue: in cases when the mother is bilingual, or if the role of mother is divided among more than one person, speaking different languages, the first linguistic input the child receives is bilingual or even multilingual.

Sometimes the term "mother tongue" is replaced by the term "first language" (e.g. see Crystal 1994: 368), which avoids inaccuracy when the mother is not the first carer of the child and denotes, in a similar way to the interpretation mentioned above, the language(s) the child learns first.

There are two more terms that are also sometimes used instead of the term "mother tongue": "dominant language" and "home language". The former denotes the language which becomes dominant in a particular environment or situation. And although in monolingual societies the child's mother tongue often remains its dominant language, in many multilingual or multidialectal societies this is not so. For example, members of the Slovene indigenous minority in Austrian Carinthia have their first linguistic input in Slovene, but then often shift to German in school and later on at work. Slovene is thus usually gradually relegated to childhood experience and German is used in all other situations. In this case, then, the Slovene language still remains dominant at home, while German assumes this role in other situations and environments. The term "home language" denotes the language a person uses at home when communicating with his/her family. This language can be completely different from (as in the case of Carinthian Slovenes who tend to use their own dialect) or the same as the public standard code of the language.

However, the general usage of the term "mother tongue" (i.e. the usage we are most interested in, because it has also been adopted in Translation Studies) denotes not only the language one learns from one's mother, but also the speaker's dominant and home language, i.e. not only the first language according to the time of acquisition, but the first with regard to its importance and the speaker's ability to master its linguistic and communicative aspects. For example, if a language school advertises that all its teachers are native speakers of English, we would most likely complain if we later learned that although the teachers do have some vague childhood memories of the time when they talked to their mothers in English, they, however, grew up in some non-English speaking country and are fluent in a second language only. Similarly, in translation theory, the claim that one should translate only into one's mother tongue, is in fact a claim that one should only translate into one's first and dominant language.

The vagueness of the term has led some researchers to claim (e.g. Tove Skutnabb-Kangas in Robert Phillipson 1989:450–477; see also Phillipson 1992:39) that different connotative meanings of the term "mother tongue" vary according to the intended usage of the word and that differences in understanding the term can have far-reaching and often political consequences. They argue that criteria for the definition of the concept depend on the hidden agenda of the one providing the definition and that they are thus likely to differ considerably and can even be contradictory. For example, these are some of the most common criteria and definitions found in linguistics:

CRITERION	DEFINITION
Origin	The language(s) one learned first.
Competence	The language(s) one knows best.
Function	The language(s) one uses most.
Identification	
– internal	The language(s) one identifies with.
– external	The language(s) of which one is identified as a native speaker by others.

Despite their extensive use, none of these criteria defines the concept of "mother tongue" objectively and completely; every definition necessarily reflects the original cultural, political and personal experience and expectations of the one providing the definition. And very often, these expectations vary considerably from those of the speakers defined and classified by such definitions. For example, the criterion of origin can be used to discriminate against second generation immigrants, who would like to be granted the status of native speaker in their new linguistic community. Their second language is often the language they count in, dream in, write their diary in and use in conscious inner speech; however, if the first criterion of origin is applied, they are considered as native speakers of only the language their parents spoke, even if they can barely understand it.

The second criterion of competence and the third criterion of function could be used to discriminate against indigenous minorities. These definitions, which are often a result of political decisions, can be used to ignore the rights of and exclude all those who are by origin native speakers of a minority language in order to deny them the opportunity to use and develop their mother tongue (see Phillipson 1992: 39). The members of a linguistic minority are quite often more proficient in the language of the majority and also use the language of their environment more often. In fact, if we adopt these criteria in legislation, minority groups could be seen as gradually completely losing their mother tongue, since children in a foreign environment, watching TV programmes in the foreign language, attending school or day care where this foreign language is employed, use their mother tongue less often than the language of the new community and therefore have poor proficiency in their mother tongue.

The fourth criterion of identification, internal and external, probably most often creates tensions, especially in the case of the post-colonial independent development of the languages of colonisers: for example, native speakers of a peripheral English-speaking community, i.e. speakers of one variety of English developed in former British colonies (of the so-called new varieties of English or the World Englishes, e.g. Indian English) are often denied the status of native speakers of English by native speakers of a core variety or the metropolitan English variety (e.g. British native speakers). Here the native speaker question is accompanied by the question of the existence of various Englishes – is there only one English or are there more? Are other Englishes only corrupt versions of the "proper English"? Which English is an Indian English speaker a native speaker of? For some speakers, answers to these questions can be vital – a case has been recorded of an English-speaking Indian who considered himself a native speaker of English because this was the only language he used, but who was not accepted as a teacher at a language school in Great Britain on the grounds that he did not comply with the advertised criteria, in particular with the condition that all candidates should be English native speakers.

This last criterion, of identification, touches upon another controversial issue in linguistics, which was largely triggered by the emergence of more than one variant of English and French in colonial settings: i.e. a decision has to be taken when a particular variety of the language is granted the status of a new language. Contemporary linguists approach the problem of the existence of different variants of English in different ways. The "traditional approach", embodied by Sir Randolph Quirk, distinguishes between native and non-native varieties of English. The latter including Indian English, Nigerian English, East African English, i.e. variants of English that developed during and after the period of the British Empire, but also Russian English, French English, Japanese English, etc., i.e. variants of English that developed in countries where English is used as an international link language. On the other hand, the native varieties cover American English, Australian English, New Zealand English, South African English, Yorkshire English etc. According to Quirk, only two of the native varieties are institutionalised: American English and British English, while there are one or two others with standards somewhat informally established, in particular Australian English (Quirk 1990: 6–7). Such a distinction led to the obvious conclusion that all native speakers of a non-native variety of English are not native speakers of English and are therefore denied any right to define the correctness or appropriateness of a particular expression in English.

The opposite view is represented by "liberation linguistics", which claims that languages or new varieties of English that developed in various peripheral English-speaking communities are new and independent languages, and should therefore not be governed by the norms of the core English-speaking communities (Kachru 1991: 3–13). Native speakers of those new varieties are therefore considered native speakers of English, i.e. of their variety of English, e.g. Indian English. The tension still persists when the core English-speaking community attempts to impose its norms on new varieties of English or when members of peripheral English-speaking communities represent themselves in core English-speaking communities as native speakers of English. And indeed, the question remains whether a native speaker of, for example Indian English, could also be used as an arbiter of acceptability in British English or American English (the role which is usually denied to them), and vice-versa, whether the native speakers of the core English-speaking countries can define the norm for the peripheral English-speaking communities (the role which is usually usurped by them). There is no doubt, however, as Davies reminds us (Davies 2003: 159), that the "traditional" attitude is similar to the attitude of British colonizers: the attitude that allowed the colonised "natives" to remain native, that accorded them large measures of local autonomy but which took for granted that it was never going to be possible for the colonised to become British.

To conclude, the definition of the term "mother tongue" depends on what those providing the definition and those defined by it want to achieve or express. All the criteria and definitions provided by linguists can be used to discriminate against one of the minority groups in the community. The concept "mother tongue" is thus not an objectively defined term which is unequivocally understood by users, and the issue is further complicated by the fact that according to the above-mentioned criteria (with the exception of the first criterion of origin), speakers can have more than one mother tongue and can even change it during their lifetime.

Defining the term "native speaker"

The concept "native speaker" has, like the term "mother tongue", more than one meaning.[2] It can be used to define a person who uses his/her mother tongue or first language, but also someone who uses his/her dominant or home language, sometimes all four at once, and sometimes only one of them. The concept of "native speaker" is defined according to different criteria, and in this case again, there is no objective definition of the concept which would cover all potential native speakers and not only the majority of them. Although there are many different definitions of a native speaker used in linguistics, all eventually turn out to be defective to a lesser or greater degree. Let us look at some of them:

1. *A native speaker of L1 is someone who has native-like intuitions by virtue of nativity.*

In this case, the status of L1 native speaker is given to those who were born in a family where L1 is spoken. The concept is defined in terms of mode of acquisition rather than of level of proficiency – which means that this criterion does not guarantee that native speakers are also proficient users of the language. Of course, in the majority of cases when the child is not only born in the country where L1 is spoken but also in a L1 family or community and lives in that community all his/her life, then the definition of origin is enough to guarantee the quality of the language used. However, the language competence and proficiency might be questionable when the child is born into a closed foreign-speaking minority group and may never achieve a native-like competence in the language of the majority. L1 proficiency might also not be attained when the child is born in the country where L1 is spoken but changes its domicile and moves to a foreign linguistic community, never using L1 again, especially if its parents become bilingual and start using the language of the new community at home. The definition is problematic also if the child is born in a peripheral L1 country, because the core country might not grant such speakers the status of native speakership.

2. *A native speaker is someone who acquired L1 during childhood in an L1-speaking family or environment* (see e.g. Bussmann 1996:320).

In this case, the criterion of environment is added to the non-linguistic criterion of birth. Again, this "bio-developmental definition" (see Davies 1996:156) does not guarantee language proficiency. For example, children who, with their families, change linguistic community and become immersed in the new language where they completely "forget" or rather neglect their mother tongue and replace it with the language of the new community might never achieve native-like competence in their mother tongue. Their mother tongue is relegated to home situations, while the foreign language is used when communicating with peers in day care or school or at work. The definition is further complicated by the fact that, like the criterion of origin, it allows a speaker to have more than one mother tongue, and it is difficult to define the linguistic environment of children who come from linguistically-mixed marriages, and grow up using two languages. If one of the parents uses L1 and the other L2 and if the child moves from the country where L1 is spoken to L2 country is then the child a native speaker of L1, of L2 or both?

3. *A native speaker is someone who uses the language creatively*

Creativity is undoubtedly one of the signs of the proficient use of language. However, even non-native speakers can sometimes use their foreign language creatively, even at an elementary stage. Moreover, some non-natives achieve exceptional results in their foreign language: for example, Joseph Conrad and Vladimir Nabokov were never granted the status of English native speakers by the English-speaking community but their works were, nevertheless, accepted as classic works of English literature. Joseph Conrad is a particularly extraordinary case – English was his third language, after Polish and French. He was born in Poland, went to live in Marseilles at seventeen, and started English at twenty while a seaman on a Polish ship. But despite this extremely late start, he became one of the leading novelists writing in English; his command of the written language placed him in the front rank of English writers and he developed superb stylistic subtlety. On the other hand, he retained a very strong foreign accent, so that even his friends had difficulty understanding him. Ford Madox Ford, for example, claimed that: "speaking English, he had so strong a French accent (sic!) that few who did not know him well could understand him at first" (Cook 1996:111). Virginia Woolf added that Conrad was "a foreigner, talking broken English", H. G. Wells that "he spoke English strangely", and Bertrand Russell that "he spoke English with a very strong foreign accent" (Cook 1996:111). It is obvious then that English native speakers did not accept him as a native speaker of English but they did, however, highly value his literary work and made him one the leading English authors of his time.

Vladimir Nabokov was also regarded by the English-speaking community as a foreigner but at the same time as one of its greatest authors. Nabokov was aware of the fact that his spoken English was considered substandard and therefore refused to lecture or be interviewed extemporaneously – he insisted on writing out every word beforehand with the help of dictionaries and grammars (see Pinker 1994:291).

Not only English, also French native speakers seem to have accepted creative writings by selected foreigners. The Czech-born Milan Kundera, for example, who moved to France in his late forties, received in 2001 the Goncourt Prize for his novel *L'Immortalité,* written in French, which undoubtedly shows his acceptance by the French public. And last but not least, to mention a translator, André Lefevere, despite retaining a distinct accent in his English, nevertheless successfully published his theoretical works in that language, translated from French, Dutch, Latin and German, and managed, according to his American colleagues at the University of Texas, to maintain the style in all the languages he translated texts into (Faulkner 2000). This ability of foreigners to master written language and to attain this skill later in life is particularly interesting for our study, since it proves that a strong accent does not represent an impediment to the successful written transfer of a text.

4. *A native speaker is someone who has the capacity to produce fluent, spontaneous discourse in English and intuitively distinguishes between correct and incorrect forms of English* (see e.g. Crystal 1992:50).

This definition, in which the mode of acquisition is judged less important than the level of proficiency attained, is most common in linguistics. In fact, even those scholars who try to avoid definitions as such and resort only to formulations of typical expectations they have of native speakers, such as Alan Davies in his *The Native Speaker in Applied Linguistics,* cannot avoid mentioning internalised rules of use and the automatic feeling that native speakers are supposed to possess:

> Let me say what I expect of the native speaker. I expect the native speaker to
> have internalised rules of use, the appropriate use of language, to know when
> to use what and how to speak to others. I expect control of strategies and
> of pragmatics, an automatic feeling for the connotations of words, for folk
> etymologies, for what is appropriate to various domains, for the import of
> a range of speech acts, in general for appropriate membership behaviour in
> him/herself and of implicit – and very rapid – detection of others as being or
> not being members.   (Davies 1991:94)

But linguistic proficiency, automatic feeling, spontaneity and intuition, so
often used with the term "native speaker", are very hard to define and even
harder to measure, especially because, as with creativity discussed above,
a certain degree of spontaneity and intuition can be found even among
beginners.

The definition regarding proficiency and competence also gives rise to a
number of further questions concerning the abilities of the native speaker, for
example: Is the "native speaker" also infallible, can s/he always intuitively distinguish between the correct and incorrect, acceptable and unacceptable forms
in a particular language? Is the native speaker an omniscient arbiter who has
access to the correct usage of the language, or not, and consequently is s/he
the one who will undoubtedly create linguistically impeccable translations? In
linguistics and in Translation Studies it sometimes seems that s/he can – the
native speaker, most probably under the influence of transformational gen-
erative grammar, is often defined as the representative ideal speaker/listener
of a linguistic community, someone who has the most reliable, even infallible, intuitions regarding the language and whose judgements about the way
the language is used can therefore be trusted. If the native speaker is competent, which usually means educated, then s/he can be used not only as an
authoritative source of judgements of grammaticality, but also as the model
for grammar.

A possible grounding for the expectations qualifying the "native speaker"
as one who has insight into a specified language or enjoys an intuitive sense of
what is grammatical and ungrammatical in regard to its usage, as someone
whose native instincts qualify him/her as a touchstone in linguistic matters
relating to a language (see e. g. Paikeday 1985:13) can indeed be found in Noam
Chomsky's *Aspects of the Theory of Syntax,* where he states that:

> A grammar is ... descriptively adequate to the extent that it correctly describes
> the intrinsic competence of the idealised native speaker. The structural de-
> scriptions assigned to sentences by the grammar, the distinctions that it makes
> between well-formed and deviant, and so on, must, for descriptive adequacy,

correspond to the linguistic intuition of the native speaker (whether or not he
may be aware of this) in a substantial and significant class of crucial cases.

(Chomsky 1965: 24)

This mythical description of an ideal native speaker, which could be deduced
from Chomsky's theoretical position, has often been attacked as an idealisation
which does not correspond to reality. But since the notion of "native speaker"
seems to be one of the fundamental concepts in Chomsky's theoretical work,
the Canadian lexicographer of Indian origin Thomas M. Paikeday decided to
discuss this issue directly with the great linguist himself. In his reply, Chomsky
associated the understanding of the concept "native speaker" with that of the
concepts "language" and "dialect".

> So then what is a language and who is a native speaker? Answer, a language
> is a system of L-s, it is the steady state attained by the language organ. And
> everyone is a native speaker of the particular L-s that that person has "grown"
> in his/her mind/brain. In the real world, that is all there is to say.
>
> (Chomsky in Paikeday 1985: 58)

This interpretation of the concepts is profoundly consistent with Chomsky's
general views, so that it is hard to argue against his position without calling into
question quite a few tenets of those views. Chomsky's position is quite clear:
he argues that every person is born with a genetically determined language
faculty (L-0) or language organ. This faculty is identical across the species (if
we ignore pathological cases), so that we can speak of the initial state L-0 of
that organ which is common to humans but also unique to the human species,
and it then undergoes changes and soon reaches a fairly steady state (L-s)
which then remains essentially unchanged apart from minor modifications.
The development of this faculty or organ, according to Chomsky, is almost
entirely completed in childhood:

> In early childhood, the organ (the language faculty or the language organ)
> undergoes changes through experience and reaches a relatively stable steady
> state L-s, probably before puberty: afterwards, it normally undergoes only
> marginal changes, like adding vocabulary.   (Chomsky in Paikeday 1985: 55)[3]

Chomsky makes a parallel between the concept of a "native speaker" and those
of "language" and "dialects", arguing that the "language" and "dialects" do
not exist as such, which means that they do not exist *in abstracto*; in the real
world there are only various states of L-s attained by various individuals. Every
individual is born with a language organ or faculty which could be developed
to a defined, genetically determined steady state. This faculty, however, does
not develop independently of the environment; the state attained does not

only depend on genetic endowment but also on experience, which defines the character of the steady state attained and the state to which the language organ or faculty will develop (ibid.: 56–57). However, everyday use of the terms demands a certain degree of simplification:

> (...) the scientific description is too precise to be useful for ordinary purposes, so we abstract from it and speak of "languages", "dialects", etc., when people are "close enough" in the steady states attained to be regarded as identical for practical purposes. (Chomsky in Paikeday 1985:60)

Chomsky argues that at a particular level individual versions of language draw so closely together that they are considered identical. Groups of people who share similar states of language thus form linguistic communities. At that point Chomsky warns us that the ordinary usage of the terms "language" and "native speaker" often goes too far and becomes too abstract and complex, especially when the terms no longer denote only a particular linguistic community but also a particular state or nationality. People tend to uncritically transfer a particular general concept used for scientific purposes to everyday, concrete situations. And when the terms "language" and "native speaker" no longer mean only a particular tool used for communication or a person with a particular steady state attained, but also a symbol of social identification, those concepts, according to Chomsky, acquire ontological implications.

Despite Chomsky's insistence that every generalisation as well as too rigid concretisation are dangerous, we can find both of them in his *Syntactic Structures*, where he talks about an ideal native speaker with a stable steady state L-s ,who with his intuitive knowledge guarantees the acceptability of grammar, in particular English grammatical structures:

> One way to test the adequacy of a grammar proposed for L is to determine whether or not the sequences that it generates are actually grammatical, i.e. acceptable to a native speaker ... (Chomsky 1957:13)

If Chomsky insisted on the claim that every speaker is a native speaker of his/her particular steady state (L-s) attained by the language organ in his mind, then he should not call upon the native speaker as an arbiter on grammaticality for a particular linguistic community, in particular, an arbiter on the grammaticality of English. Moreover, would it be sensible to describe syntactic structures pertaining to the steady state attained by the language organ of one individual only? Indeed, in the above-quoted sentence Chomsky, it seems, is not talking about a concrete speaker but about an ideal native speaker who could be used as a touchstone for the grammaticality of phrases and sentences of the entire linguistic community and not only of his/her individual language variety, i.e. for the normative English language and not for the speaker's idiosyncratic variant of it. Most probably he would argue that the steady state attained by the language organ of this particular speaker is "very close" to those of other speakers who form a linguistic community of English (despite the fact that he warns us against over-generalisations) – but we are still left with the unanswered question as to what the range of the criterion "close enough" covers and what deviations are still acceptable in order to consider a speaker a member of a particular linguistic community.

Chomsky is undoubtedly right when he claims, if we simplify his reply, that all people are native speakers of whatever they have learned, and that their particular variety of the language, however, is in many features similar to the varieties of other members of their linguistic community – this very similarity and compatibility of their individual variants enables successful communication, and communication is usually, after all, the aim of using a language. As far as the existence of different varieties of English is concerned, his answers can be understood to imply that, for example, an Indian speaker of English could be considered a native speaker of Indian English but also that all Indian speakers are not "close enough" to the steady states attained by the speakers of metropolitan English variety. But the crucial questions for our study still remain unanswered: which speakers are considered "close enough" and which are not? Is it possible that some speakers are left outside, and should not therefore be considered as competent and proficient enough, as arbiters on grammaticality of the linguistic community they were born into? Chomsky does not give an answer to that; he does, however, seem to imply that the status of native speakership should be given only to those who attained the steady state of the language organ before puberty, which means that this linguistic competence expected from native speakers, the ability to use the language correctly, cannot be acquired later in life.

Other theoreticians, on the other hand, raise doubts as to whether the element of origin, stressed by the term "native speaker", is indeed such an important factor for making a distinction between well-formed and deviant forms. Rampton (1990:100), for example, argues that all speakers born in a particular linguistic community do not have highly developed knowledge of the language, even though this language might be the only one they use, and that therefore nationality and ethnicity are not the same as language ability, since they do not guarantee that the speaker is also competent in that particular language.

But even if we modify our understanding of the concept of "native speaker" and with Paikeday (1985:40, 87) claim that a native speaker is a competent

speaker of a particular language who can use this language idiomatically–
where idiomatically means "the usual way in which the words of a particular
language are joined together to express thought" or "the syntactical, grammatical, or structural form peculiar to a language" (Paikeday 1985: 10) – and
thus avoid the element of origin, there still remains the problem of distinction
between competent and less-competent speakers of a particular language.

To test intuition is almost impossible – the nature of the subject by
definition escapes every schematisation. But despite the difficulty of the task,
there have been some attempts in the field of psycholinguistics to draw a
line between native and non-native speakers of a particular language. Thus
René Coppieters attempted to define the native/non-native distinction and
to pinpoint these differences in intuitive choices between native speakers and
near-native speakers of French. He carried out his experiment on 20 native
speakers of French and 21 adult near-native speakers who had all acquired
French as adults and had not used the language for normal communicative
purposes before the age of 18. The near-native speakers all lived in France
and had been using French for at least five years in everyday communication,
while the mean residence level was 17 years. Coppieters chose only those
subjects that were believed by French native speakers to be as linguistically and
communicatively proficient in French as native speakers.

The questionnaire tested the distribution of the anaphoric uses of the third
person pronouns *il/elle* and *ce* in predicative sentences; the subjects were asked
to choose the right location for different adjectives according to the meaning of
the sentence, they had to make tense and aspect distinctions (*passé composé* vs.
imparfait), decide on the right preposition (*à* vs. *de + infinitive*), decide among
different articles and use the correct form in complex syntactical structures.
The results of the study showed that all near-native speakers had a greater need
for an explicit context in order to derive the appropriate interpretation of a
sentence and that none of the near-native speakers interviewed could be taken
as having developed interpretative intuitions comparable to those of the native
speakers of French (Coppieters 1987: 566–568).

Further research seems to suggest other areas of non-native "weaknesses";
e.g. some studies show that collocation errors and the absence of idiomatic
phrasing are typical of the non-native speakers' writings. Late starters also
do not seem to be able to achieve native competence in such subtle areas
as culturally appropriate topic choice and other conversational strategies (see
Long 1990: 273). The findings of the study by Georgette Ioup and her colleagues
where an adult (Julie) was investigated who seemed to have acquired native
proficiency in her foreign language (Egyptian Arabic) in an untutored setting

is particularly interesting for Translation Studies, since in assessing Julie's level of achievement Ioup also tested her translation abilities. Julie's results were compared to those of a proficient learner (Laura) of Egyptian Arabic with extensive formal instruction. Nor surprisingly, their grammar and morphology were flawless. However, once they both used a preposition wrongly, and Julie in one instance did not make the right word order distinction (see Ioup et al. 1994: 82–83). They both came very close to a native level of proficiency in perceptual abilities, production skills, and underlying linguistic competence; however, in the domain of discourse syntax and semantics they failed to reach native norms (Ioup et al. 1994: 91).

On the other hand, other studies have demonstrated that some L2 users are nevertheless indistinguishable from native speakers in syntax and even phonology (see Cook 1999: 191). Furthermore, Birdsong re-examined the Coppieters' experiment and contrary to Coppieter's findings concluded that ultimate attainment by non-natives can coincide with that of natives (Birdsong 1992: 739), of course, only in the case of "exceptional learners". Similarly Davies' replications of Ross' study (1979) and the Eisenstein and Bodman (1986) study show that both in grammaticality judgements and in pragmatic selections, in certain cases, individual non-native speakers are indistinguishable from native speakers (Davies 2003: 186–194). Those studies, however, document the achievements of a few exceptional learners who through education and training became native speakers of the target language (see Davies 2003: 192).

The majority of second language users/learners, however, never achieve that level in their target language. The empirical evidence show that in the majority of cases the speakers who move to a new linguistic community after puberty do not attain the same level of connectedness with the new language as native speakers, which would allow them to intuitively differentiate more appropriate forms from less appropriate ones. In other words, in general if speakers move to a new linguistic community in adulthood, it is already too late for them to develop native-like intuitions for the language.

But is it possible to develop native-like competence if a person moves to a new linguistic community before adulthood and when precisely is it too late? The vast majority of linguists think that it is possible and remain convinced that the length of residence and frequency of exposure to a foreign language, combined with the fact that a particular person came in contact with the foreign language *early* in his/her childhood, enables the speaker to develop an intuition comparable to that of a competent native speaker of that language. However, it is added, the person should move to the new linguistic environment before the so-called critical period or sensitive periods decisive for language acquisition.

Which age is the optimum age for acquiring native-speaker competence in a language? When answering this question we touch upon another heated debate in applied linguistics: the discussion of whether the same fundamental process controls both the child's learning of a first language and the adult's learning of a foreign language (e.g. Dulay, Burt, & Krashen 1982: 200–229), or whether there are two processes involved. Traditionally, the latter is believed: i.e. that child language development and adult foreign language learning are in fact fundamentally different. Differences between two kinds of language learning, those of adults and those of children, are described with two different terms: language learning and language acquisition. The adults are supposed to *learn* the language, i.e. consciously learn explicit grammatical rules, while children are supposed to *acquire* the language, i.e. unconsciously internalise a knowledge of language by using the language naturally in communicative situations (Bley-Vroman 1990: 5; Yule 1985: 151). Unfortunately, conscious memorisation of grammar is held not to be the same thing as developing real language competence. Most probably because adults have the advantage (which becomes an impediment in this case) of having perfect knowledge of at least one language, their mother tongue, they approach a foreign-language differently to children – for them, it is an instance of general adult problem-solving, and they are less successful at this task (see also Cook 1999: 193).

On the other hand, this general lack of complete success with adult learners of foreign language is argued by some scholars to be a result of other factors and not of the fact that adults learn a foreign language differently than children. Krashen, for example, claims that adults, besides having the ability to learn, continue to use the same language-specific acquisition processes which allow children to develop their feel for the language (Krashen 1982: 10). He is convinced that the adult way of acquisition is in fact identical to that of children when they acquire their first language, as they both have access to the same language acquisition device:

> Some second language theorists have assumed that children acquire, while adults can only learn. The acquisition-learning hypothesis claims, however, that adults also acquire, that the ability to "pick up" languages does not disappear at puberty. This does not mean that adults will always be able to achieve native-like levels in a second language. It does mean that adults can access the same natural "language acquisition device" that children use.
>
> (Krashen 1982: 10)

Adults and children may use the same language faculty or organ when learning a language; the empirical evidence shows, however, that children, and only children, uniformly succeed in learning language (see e.g. Newport 1990:27). And although adults and older beginners initially progress faster than those who start learning a foreign language in early childhood, they almost never achieve complete success, while younger learners tend to catch up with adults and eventually outstrip them (cf. Cook 1996:112–113; Singleton 1992:47; Long 1990:260). Moreover, numerous linguists insist that those children who were born in the foreign country develop a full grammatical system in the second language and in that sense become indistinguishable from those who have had only one language input since birth (see e.g. Davies 1991:64). That means that children of immigrants who were born in the foreign country become native speakers of the new linguistic community. The question remains as to what happens to the children who were born in the country of their parents and moved with them to a new linguistic community – do they also become native speakers of the new language? In other words: which age is crucial for language acquisition or when is it too late for a child to become a native speaker of a new linguistic community?

Children's first language acquisition is undoubtedly age-related; no one is born with a language, and the majority of people (putting aside pathology, injury, etc.) learn the basics of at least one language by age 3 or 4. Some linguists emphasise that towards the age of three there is a major grammatical advance, with the appearance of sentences containing more than one clause. However, the process of acquisition does not stop at that age; some recent studies have shown that the acquisition of several types of construction is still taking place as children approach the age of 11 or 12 (Crystal 1994:245).

There appears to be one or more sensitive periods also for second language acquisition, with approximately the same lower and upper age bounds as those for first language development. Thus the ability to attain native-like phonological abilities in a second language begins to decline by age 6 in the majority of individuals and seems very hard to attain for those beginning later than age 12, no matter how motivated they might be or how much opportunity they might have. Native-like morphology and syntax seem to be possible for the majority of the speakers if they begin before age 15, and somewhere in between these ages for the remaining linguistic domains (see Long 1990:274, 280).

It seems, then, that the optimum age for acquiring native speaker competence is before puberty. The majority of children relatively easy "pick up" language at that period and attain such a competence, provided that they are in constant contact with this language, or somehow "immersed" in it. On the other hand, children who get in touch with a foreign language at puberty more often retain their foreign accent and very rarely achieve a level of proficiency comparable to that of native speakers.

An attempt was made in the mid-twentieth century to explain these differences in linguistic competence and proficiency with the process of lateralisation of the brain. Since it was found that with certain species (e.g. rats, goslings) there were periods, so-called critical periods, in which a particular kind of stimulus had to be present if the baby was to develop normal behaviour (Crystal 1994:263), it has also been argued that there are critical periods in human maturation, in particular in the case of language acquisition. Thus in 1967, the American psycholinguist Eric H. Lenneberg (1921–1975) first hypothsised that there was a biologically-active period of language development, the so-called critical period, extending from infancy to perhaps puberty, when the child has to acquire its mother tongue. This period was considered so crucial because it was argued that up to adolescence lateralisation is not yet complete, i.e. the two hemispheres of the cerebral cortex have not yet acquired specialisation of function that characterises the adult brain – in particular, the left hemisphere has not yet specialised for language. Lenneberg was convinced that, in accordance with the findings of the neurophysiologist W. G. Penfield (Stern 1983:326), at birth both hemispheres of the cerebral cortex were equally strong and not yet specialised, which means that lateralisation was not yet complete. He came to this conclusion by observing pre-pubertal children who had suffered brain damage in the speech area of the cerebral cortex through accidents, brain tumours, and surgical intervention, and found out that they recovered speech better than adolescents or adults by using the right hemisphere, which seems impossible after the puberty. Lenneberg therefore assumed that the brain's hemispheric specialisation for language is not achieved until about the time of puberty, which coincided with the ending of the critical period for language acquisition. The critical period is thus the period after which the child is no longer capable of naturally acquiring the language and thus also attaining the proficiency of the native speaker (see Krashen 1981:72; Stern 1983:362; Cook 1996:108).

A number of other investigators have pursued Lenneberg's hypothesis – the most notable example was the study of the tragic case of a girl called Genie. Genie was born in a Los Angeles suburb where she spent thirteen years and a half in complete isolation, until she was discovered and rescued in 1970 from her psychotic father. Genie's father could not tolerate any noise and therefore tied his daughter to a chair in a room which was visited only by her mother, who brought her food. Genie grew up completely isolated from linguistic input and all other normal societal and environmental stimulation. When she was later taught to speak, she developed abnormal linguistic competence (Curtiss 1977) and produced sentences like: "Mike paint. Applesauce buy store. Neal come happy; Neal not come sad. I like elephant eat peanut," (Pinker 1994: 292).

The case of Genie only partly supported Lenneberg's hypothesis: Genie did, despite her late start, nevertheless develop a certain language facility and communicated linguistically (although abnormally) with her environment. She used the right hemisphere for this task instead of the left one (Yule 1985: 133; Crystal 1994: 263), which provided evidence that the human brain is not completely specialised by the end of puberty and that the ability to acquire a language does not completely vanish after that period.

The assumption that age is an important factor in mother tongue acquisition was additionally strengthened by two other cases. The first case was the case of a girl called "Isabelle", who at the age of six and a half escaped with her mute and brain-damaged mother from her grandfather, who had kept them imprisoned in silent isolation. Although she was not able to talk when she escaped, a year and a half later she became extremely skilful in English in acquired between 1500 to 2000 words (Pinker 1994: 292). A different outcome has been reported for the second case, that of "Chelsea". Chelsea was a woman whose deafness was not recognised at birth, and thus grew up languageless to the age of 31, when her medical condition was diagnosed. But despite auditory amplification, Chelsea never achieved normal linguistic competence in any language (Curtiss 1988) and formed sentences as: "The small a the hat. Richard eat peppers hot. Orange Tim car in. Banana the eat," (Pinker 1994: 293). Isabelle was able to learn the language properly, while Chelsea was not, and this change in the level of success attained was attributed to the age difference of the two subjects.

The question still remains whether the reported cases were not too exceptional to be used as explanations of the usual course of development of language learning and language acquisition. For example, Genie did not only grow up languageless, she also lived in complete sensory deprivation and sustained considerable emotional scars during her confinement, she was brought up in conditions of inhuman neglect and extreme isolation, not only was she not talked to, she heard almost no sound and experienced no love and physical contact. She was severely disturbed and underdeveloped (cf. Crystal 1994: 263) and all these factors surely interfered with her ability to learn.

And indeed, Lenneberg's attempt to explain the critical period with a neurological mechanism has not been supported by subsequent work, and studies of healthy children in a normal environment contradicted many of

Lenneberg's conjectures. The neuropsychological evidence generally shows that laterilisation is established long before puberty, at the age of five, some studies even suggest that this may even be as early as the third year, while certain preconditions for lateralisation, like cerebral anatomical and functional asymmetries, are already present at birth (Krashen 1981:73–76).

On the other hand, it is obvious that it takes some years before lateralisation is firmly established and that the important cognitive and affective changes accelerating the development of the ability to learn a foreign language and, at the same time, decelerating the ability to acquire language, happen during puberty. Although some scholars argue that although after puberty children learn foreign languages with more difficulty and are less successful, this is not connected with the process of lateralisation of the brain or any other neuro-physiological changes, and that the ability to acquire a language is never completely lost (Krashen 1981); it is also true that the period of the establishment of lateralisation overlaps with the main period of language acquisition – which means that the complexity of the possible relationship between lateralisation and language acquisition still needs to be resolved.

Thus contemporary linguistics offers conflicting views: some linguists are convinced that pre-pubescent children are in effect better language learners than adolescents and adults, others disagree and claim that adults are often superior to children in learning a foreign language (except in acquiring an acceptable accent) (Stern 1983:363) and argue that adolescents can achieve great success in foreign language learning (Yule 1985:151). A representative of the latter group is, for example, Robert Bley-Vroman, who argues:

> Teenagers, interestingly, often seem to achieve native-speaker competence. Indeed, some studies show that in the age range of 10 to 15, they not only reach native-speaker competence, but they also progress more rapidly and perform with greater accuracy in the early stages of learning than do their younger counterparts.   (Bley-Vroman 1990:9)

Quite a few scholars (for a survey see Littlewood 1984:66–67, also Singleton 1992:47) provide evidence that more mature students are much more successful in language learning, in particular when learning grammar, but lag behind in phonetics:

> Indeed, the weight of evidence suggests that, given more or less equal opportunities, efficiency in second language learning increases with age, and that younger learners are superior only in acquiring pronunciation skills.
>   (Littlewood 1984:66)

Some linguists therefore wanted to ascertain whether children, e.g. children of immigrants, are indeed more successful in acquiring a new language than their parents and whether there are any differences between those who start in their early childhood and those who start in their teens. For this purpose Elissa L. Newport (1990) and her colleagues designed a grammaticality judgement test which consisted of a list of simple English sentences, half of them containing some grammatical error and tested subjects whose first language was Chinese or Korean and who had spent at least 10 years in the United States. They wanted to examine whether the age of onset of acquisition is related to performance in the language, i.e. whether the maturational state affects the learning of the second language. The results supported the thesis that younger learners outstrip older ones. The immigrants who came to the U.S. as small children, between the ages of 3 and 7, achieved results in the test which were identical to those of American-born students. The immigrants who arrived between the ages of 8 and 15 did increasingly worse the later they arrived, and the quality of their performance declined in correlation with the age of their arrival – the older they were the worse they performed. Those who arrived between 17 and 39 did the worst of all, but the quality of their performance was unrelated to the age of their arrival in the U.S., and seems to have been the result of different individual capacities.

Similar results were provided by studies of immigrants to West Germany (see Littlewood 1984:65) and confirmed the assumption that the younger the person is on arrival in the new country, the more proficient s/he is likely to become in the language. Moreover, linguists seem to have accepted the assumption that the children of immigrants who were born in a new country are at least bilingual if not native speakers of the language of the new linguistic community, which means that they are supposed to be equally competent in their new language as monolingual native speakers (see e.g. Eisenstein and Bodman 1986:174).

On the other hand, in the 1990's some studies were conducted with exceptional learners where non-native speakers fell within the range of native speaker performance on a grammaticality judgement tasks (see Birdsong 1992) and were able to attain English pronunciation ratings within the same range as those attained by native speakers (see Bongaerts, Planken, & Schils 1995). The weight of evidence thus suggests that for the majority of the population the greatest success is achieved by the least mature learners, which is in contrast to most cognitive domains, where children are much less capable than adults. However, some exceptionally gifted individuals may acquire native-speaker competence also later in life.

The reasons for such a situation are numerous and linguists have identified only some of them: affective, input, cognitive, and neurological variables are usually used to explain the general decline in language learning ability. Unfortunately, they all appear insufficient in one way or another. Some scholars thus argue that affective, social and psychological factors such as attitude towards the new community, motivation, self-esteem, empathy, perceived social distance may impede second-language acquisition and stop input from reaching the brain areas responsible for language acquisition (e.g. Krashen 1982). In particular, the speaker's willingness to identify with the new linguistic group seems to be one of the crucial factors in determining the proficiency of a person in a foreign language – the need and wish to communicate may mark the success in mastering the new language. For example, an eight-year old child whose parents moved to a foreign country will most probably want and need to communicate with other children in order to survive in the new environment. If, on the other hand, the child is surrounded by other children of the minority group, where it can continue using its mother tongue, then the development of bilingualism will be slowed down (cf. Grosjean 1982: 193).

Others claim that input factors are more important; e.g. children usually have better learning conditions than older learners, they receive linguistically less complex input and have more time at their disposal, a greater communicative need and more varied opportunities to use the language. Children in schools also receive more focused attention from native speakers of the language, including other children, than their parents, they usually do not hold negative attitudes towards the new linguistic community, they have fewer inhibitions, are less embarrassed when they make mistakes, they have less fear of being rejected by the environment and usually do not analyse and apply conscious thought to learning the language, but let acquisition take its proper course (see Littlewood 1984: 66).

Some again suggest that cognitive factors are crucial, i.e. that decreasing adult language-learning ability is caused by increasing cognitive development. According to them child first-language development and second-language acquisition and adult second-language acquisition are different processes; children thus use the so-called language acquisition device or universal grammar while adults general problem-solving abilities.

And finally, the last group of linguists suggest that neurological or neurophysiological factors are the main cause of those differences, i.e. that the loss of neural plasticity which impedes successful second language acquisition is caused by lateralization, or that the plasticity loss is due to other cerebral changes like myelination, i.e. thickening of the band of white fibres that connects the cerebral hemispheres, the so-called corpus callosum (see Long 1990). Some argue that bilinguals are not simply a mental combination of two mono-linguals but represent a complex re-organisation of mental skills (see Bialystok 1998:510) and that they should not be compared to monolingual native speakers at all. In fact, Cook claims that the only occasion on which L2 users can justifiably be measured against native speakers is when they are passing for natives, for example, when making translations to be read as native rather than non-native texts (Cook 1999:196). However, although also the first results of magnetic resonance imaging seem to suggest that there exist different kinds of brain organization in early and late bilinguals (see Kim, Relking, Kyoung-Min, & Hirsch 1997), the notion that decreasing adult language-learning ability is exclusively neurologically-based and associated with absolute, well-defined chronological limits particular to language does not seem plausible (see Singleton 2001:85).

To conclude, like the notion of "mother tongue", the concept "native speaker" remains vague and unclarified in linguistics. Almost all definitions of the term exclude marginal cases, e.g. they do not take into account immigrants, children of immigrants and speakers of peripheral varieties of a particular language, which seems to strengthen the claim that these definitions are often ethnocentric and political. In particular, the assumed intuitive capacity of every native speaker to distinguish between acceptable and deviant forms of a particular language proves problematic and questionable. Some speakers, despite the fact that they were born and grew up in a monoglot community of speakers of a particular language do not master the standard code of the language. On the other hand, other studies have demonstrated that a few exceptional foreign speakers can come close to, if not even merge with, the group of native speakers of a particular language. Although it is assumed that this is more common if the child moves to a new country in early childhood, linguists have no answer to the question of when the sensitive period for acquiring a particular language occurs, i.e. they do not know the exact age when a person should be exposed to a foreign language in order to attain a fluency and competence comparable to that of native speakers. Having a language as one's first language is a decided advantage in achieving competence in it; however, it seems that native speakership is often also a question of education, individual aptitude and extralinguistic factors.

But despite these limitations, numerous translation scholars took over these terms as objectively defined and thus avoided a more complex description what translators are really like. Those terms are taken for granted and are central to many theoretical writings. They underlie some of its most persistent axiomatic truths – one of them being the conviction that that every translator should be a native speaker of the TL, i.e. that every translator should work only into his/her mother tongue in order to achieve acceptable results.

Translation into a non-mother tongue in translation theory

Challenging the traditional

Mystification of the native speaker – the translator as owner of the TL

The assumption that translators can master only their mother tongue and must therefore translate only in that direction, despite its seemingly eternal and ancient aura, developed rather late in the Western world. In fact, it seems to have been Martin Luther who in defence of his translation for the first time explicitly considered his knowledge of the TL as a decisive advantage over his critics (Luther 1963: 18–22), which led many of his readers to the conclusion that one can translate satisfactorily only into one's own language. Luther's conviction was taken over and strengthened by the first and second, nationalist generation of Romantic authors, who also made a great contribution to the rise of national philologies. The German Romantics in particular emphasised the essential connectedness of language and nation, and therefore many of their writings expressed powerful mystification of the native speaker and of the mother tongue. For example, Wilhelm von Humboldt claimed not only that the nation was deeply connected with its language, but that the nation's language was the spirit of that nation, which consequently meant that only those who spoke the language of a particular community could access the hidden essence of the nation:

> Die Sprache ist gleichsam die äußerliche Erscheinung des Geistes der Völker; ihre Sprache ist ihr Geist und ihr Geist ihre Sprache, man kann sich beide nicht identisch genug denken. (Humboldt in Stolze 1994: 24)

The translator can thus never write the way the author of the original would have written in the language of the translator (Humboldt 1977: 42) because a complete transition from one language to another is impossible. Every language has its own means of expression, which remains inaccessible to everyone who does not speak that particular language from birth. Translation should therefore always proceed from foreign languages to one's mother tongue and never vice-versa, since the hidden essence of the target language is not attainable by any foreign speaker. It seems then that the roots of the conviction that we can grasp the ungraspable only in our mother tongue, and consequently create a convincing translation only in our native language, stem from this Romantic identification of the transcendental nature of the nation and its language.

Although the belief in the transcendental connectedness of the nation and its language abated in the modern age, its logical corollary that one should always translate into one's mother tongue survived. It can thus also be found in contemporary writings on translation, for example in Peter Newmark's work where he is short but blatantly direct in regard to this same problem:

> (...) A foreigner appears to go on making collocational mistakes however long he lives in his adopted country, possibly because he has never distinguished between grammar and lexicology. (...) For the above reasons, translators rightly translate into their own language, and *a fortiori*, foreign teachers and students are normally unsuitable in a translation course.(Newmark 1981:180)

Translators should thus translate only into their mother tongues; even if a person lives in a TL culture for years, his or her writing will be, according to Newmark, "unnatural and non-native", full of "unacceptable or improbable collocations" (ibid.). Because of the practical nature of some aspects of Newmark's writings, the influence of his thought has spread to books on translation teaching and guides for translators, which also often defend the superiority of direct translations. Thus, for example, Alan Duff argues that the most frequent criticism of translation is that it does not sound natural and that this unnaturalness is in general the result of interference from the original, i.e the fact that translations are too strongly moulded by the source text (Duff 1989:11). He is convinced that words have a suggestive power that goes far beyond their dictionary value and that translation should therefore always be carried out by native speakers of the TL, since only they are capable of intuitively grasping word associations which reflect the way in which language structures and organises reality (Duff 1981:111, 125).

Geoffrey Samuelsson-Brown also repeats the axiomatic conviction that language conceals in its core undefinable components that are hidden from those who are not its native speakers:

> Yes, you may be able to translate quite correctly into a foreign language but it will eventually become evident that the translation was not written by a "native".
> (Samuelsson-Brown 1995:16)

Both Samuelsson-Brown and Duff do not define the concept of the native speaker, leaving it vague and undetermined; they do, however, repeat and strengthen the unproven assumption that native speakers structure reality differently compared to the speakers who learned or acquired language later in life and that therefore translations done by non-natives are necessarily inferior to those done by native speakers of the TL.

This traditionally indisputable stand, however, reveals considerable cracks and inevitably provokes the following questions: Who is the native speaker these theoreticians are talking about? The speaker of the core or the speaker of the peripheral variant of the language? Are the children of immigrants who are born in a foreign country also native speakers of this foreign language or not? Is a person who moved to a new linguistic environment in his/her childhood a native speaker of that new language, and if so, when does childhood stop? What about pairs of translators consisting of a native and a non-native speaker of the TL – which language is their mother tongue? Since the supporters of native superiority do not define the concept of the native speaker, despite the central position they grant to this notion in their theoretical works, their categorical claims seem more than suspect. They do not provide in support of their views any proofs concerning the greater competence and proficiency of native speakers compared to those of near-native speakers and they often ignore or downgrade the possibility of translation pairs, consisting of a native and a non-native speakers of the TL (see e.g. Samuelsson-Brown 1995:16). The advocates of this view simply take the concept of the native speaker for granted, as if its meaning is objectively defined and final, and never seem to question and theoretically challenge any of the idealisations connected with the term – for example, the assumption of the infallibility of the native speaker – despite the fact that the concept is used in such prescriptive sentences as the ones quoted above.

Some contemporary translation practicioners and theoreticians then un-critically accept the concept of an ideal native speaker as an arbiter and model of grammaticality, who masters his/her mother tongue completely and in all its details, who has access to all the hidden channels of unutterable associa-tive connectedness between words and concepts, and can therefore also create linguistically and culturally impeccable translations. This theoretical position, however, also has an additional corollary: it ethnocentrically defends the no-tion of the superiority of the "natural native speaker", the innate state that can never be acquired, and thus rejects the marginal and peripheral (i.e. trans-lators from immigrant communities and the practice of team translation) as necessarily inferior.

The idealisation of the translator – a perfect bilingual translator

The essential vagueness of the basic terms "mother tongue" and "native speaker" has most probably led another group of translation theoreticians to avoid the question as to whether translators should be native speakers of the source or of the target language altogether; instead, they have idealised the subject involved in the process of translation and assumed that translators are, or at least should be, perfect bilingual speakers of both, source and target languages, translating from one mother tongue to another.

This requirement of a perfect bilingual speaker for a successful translation, however, is not often found explicitly expressed before the period when Translation Studies entered its linguistic era. One of the rare exceptions is the German philosopher, poet, critic and translator Johann Gottfried Herder (1744–1803) who, as early as the late 18th century, claimed that the translator should not get too close to either of his two languages, i.e. to the one he translates from or to the one he translates into (Herder 1977: 33). Despite this general principle, however, Herder reveals in the same text that the languages mentioned are not completely equal and that the translator should therefore adapt words and manners of speaking from a more developed language, e.g. from Greek or Latin, and then transport them into his mother tongue (Herder in Lefevere 1992: 74) – which means that, according to Herder, the ideal bilingual translator in real life nevertheless works from his foreign language into his mother tongue.

Although rare before the 20th century, the call for a bilingual translator became very common in the linguistic current of translatological thought. We can find it, for instance, in J. C. Catford's structuralist work *A Linguistic Theory of Translation* (1965), where he claims that the "discovery of textual equivalents is based on the competent *bilingual* informant or translator" (Catford 1965: 27). However, by the end of the century, bilingualism seems to have been by-passed: translation was no longer considered as a solely linguistic event – other skills and knowledge were needed for the successful transfer of text. Thus Ernst-August Gutt (1990: 143), in his relevance theory of communication, not only demands that translators be bilingual, but also adds that since translation is a cross-cultural event (ibid.: 139) it presupposes more than just the language competence of the translator. Similarly, Roger T. Bell (1991: 15, 38, 40) claims that the ideal translator must possess, in addition to linguistic competence in both languages, communicative competence in both cultures (Bell 1991: 42).

For contemporary Translation Studies the ideal of the bilingual translator with high competence in receptive and productive skills in both languages is thus coupled with additional demands that the translator should also be bi- or even multicultural. Expertise in the cultures involved is particularly stressed by theorists belonging to the so-called cultural turn in Translation Studies: Lefevere and Bassnet, for example, even claiming that for the translator biculturality is even more important than bilingualism (Lefevere and Bassnett 1990: 11).[4]

Some scholars, however, are even more demanding: for them the ideal translator is supposed to be experienced in translation, possess grammatical, textual and pragmatic competences, but above all have broad knowledge in multiple subject areas covered by different texts (Cao 1996: 330, 337). Neubert and Shreve claim that the translator should not only be a linguistic, communicative and cultural expert, but also an expert in the economic, scientific, cultural or technical domains communicated through the original (Neubert & Shreve 1992: 38).

The influential "skopos" theory of translation also did not escape the idealisation of the translator's aptitudes. Thus Vermeer, when asked in January 1998 in Ljubljana whether the ideal translator within the framework of the "skopos" theory translates into his/her mother tongue or also vice-versa, replied that the theory does not, in fact, take this problem into consideration. The translator within the "skopos" theory is a bilingual, bicultural (maybe even multicultural) person who knows well the subject area of the original text and is therefore able to transfer it adequately to the reality of the target culture. According to Vermeer, the question of whether such a person exists or not in real life is not relevant, since every theory should operate only with abstract, ideal notions. Most probably under the influence of this theoretical position, such idealisation was then introduced into translation didactics. Thus Mary Snell-Hornby, for example, writes that the aim of all translation teaching is to create "not only a bilingual but also a bicultural (if not multicultural) specialist working with and within an infinite variety of areas of technical expertise" (Snell-Hornby 1992: 11).

However, none of these theoreticians attempts to define bilingualism or biculturalism, they just take those concepts for granted. And, as in the case of the notions of "native speaker" and "mother tongue", linguists, unfortunately, admit that the notion of "bilingualism" is theoretically unclear in evades water-tight definition. The crucial problem that remains unsolved is which level of competence and proficiency in the two languages involved defines bilingualism, since, as said before, linguistics lacks acid tests which would allow us to define the level of proficiency and competence acquired by a particular speaker. Some linguists are therefore much more prudent – Crystal, for example, avoids generalisations when describing bilingual speakers and argues that "real", i.e. perfect bilingual speakers who would master both of their languages equally well are very rare, if they exist at all:

> The notion of proficiency raises some very complex issues. Again, the obvious answer is to say that people are bilingual when they achieve native-like fluency in each language. But this criterion is far too strong. People who have "perfect" fluency in two languages do exist, but they are exception, not the rule.
>
> (Crystal 1987: 362)

Moreover, Crystal claims that bilingual speakers often do not attain the level of competence and proficiency of the native speaker in any of the languages they speak (ibid.). Bilingualism in linguistics therefore does not mean the "perfect" mastery of the two languages involved, but greater or lesser ability to communicate in both languages. Such understanding of bilingualism could also be found in post-colonial translation theory, focussing on the works of bilingual and bicultural subjects writing in their language "in between" (see e.g. Mehrez 1992, 121), which has nothing in common with the theoretical idealisations mentioned above. But not all translation theoreticians take this relativism into account: the majority still cling to the concept of the ideal bilingual and bicultural translator, despite the fact that they know that this quintessential state we all aspire to and never really attain, this idealisation of the translator's aptitudes, has no tangible reflection in real life.

A hidden traditional conviction

The most common approach to the problem of directionality in translation theory is, however, a silent acceptance of the "traditional" conviction of the necessity to translate into one's mother tongue. Most translation theoreticians do not discuss openly the possibility of choosing one's TL in translation; however, they do covertly express their conviction that only translation into one's mother tongue guarantees a good translation. This opaque discourse can already be found in the 17th and 18th centuries, for example in the preface to Ovid's *Epistles*, where John Dryden writes: "No man is capable of translating poetry, who, besides a genius to that art, is not a master of both of *his author's language, and of his own*..." (Dryden 1997: 173; emphasis added), or in Jacques

Delille's (1738–1813) writings, where he claims that with translation we import the wealth of the *foreign* language into our own (Delille 1992: 37).

The Romantics were even more determined in their claim that translators should only be members of the TL culture, partly because they regarded translation as a means to augment the significance and expressiveness of the native language (see e.g. Humboldt 1997: 239). Victor Hugo, for example, argued that every translation of a foreign author adds to the national poetry (Hugo 1992: 18) revealing that, according to him, translation is always done from a foreign language into one's mother tongue and never vice-versa. A similar conviction could also be found in the famous lecture by Friedrich Schleiermacher *Über die verschiedenen Methoden des Übersetzens* (1813), in which the author, among other things, emphasises that a translator should not allow himself anything that would not also be allowed in an original work of the same genre in *his native language* (Schleiermacher 1985: 322, emphasis added).[5] Although Schleiermacher never openly claims that the translator should translate only into his mother tongue, this conviction permeates his panegyric of the German language and culture – direct translation seems to be the only translation he envisaged.

Walter Benjamin is even more prescriptive. In his seminal text "The Task of the Translator", written as an introduction to Baudelaire's *Tableaux Parisiens* and, according to Paul de Man, one of the most important texts of Western thought (de Man 1991: 21–52), Benjamin reveals that the only possible direction of translation is from a foreign language to the translator's mother tongue:

> It is the task of the translator to release *in his own language* that pure language which is under the spell of another, to liberate the language imprisoned in a work in his re-creation of that work.   (Benjamin 1982: 80)

Benjamin, revealing the influences of German Romanticism, demands that the translator should not only master his own mother tongue but also allow the foreign language to transform the target language by means of translation and thus liberate the power of the pure, original language – and this extremely important and difficult task seems to be possible only if one is translating into one's mother tongue.

In addition to traditional writings, the hidden assumption that one always translates into one's mother tongue can also be found in contemporary theories – thus we can find it in Eillis Barnstone's work (Barnstone 1993, 109),[6] in Barbara Johnson's deconstructivist thoughts (Johnson 1985: 142),[7] in Sherry Simon's feminist work (Simon 1996: 94),[8] and in Mary Snell-Hornby's integrated approach. Although Snell-Hornby often explicitly insists on the bilin-gualism and multiculturality of the translator (e.g. Snell-Hornby 1992:11), it is obvious that the prevailing practice in the major linguistic communities never-theless influenced some of her statements. For example, in *Translation Studies: An Integrated Approach* she writes:

> The translator starts from a presented frame (the text and its linguistic components); this was produced by an author who drew from his own repertoire of partly prototypical scenes. Based on the frame of the text, the translator-reader builds up his own scenes depending on his own level of experience and his internalized knowledge of the material concerned. *As a non-native speaker*, the translator might well activate scenes that diverge from the author's intentions or deviate from those activated by a native speaker of the source language (a frequent cause of translation error).
>
> (Snell-Hornby [1988] 1995:81; emphasis added)

According to Snell-Hornby, the ideal translator, despite his/her multicultural-ity, nevertheless remains primarily the native speaker of the TL, with all the limitations and advantages such a position entails.

This hidden discourse on directionality is particularly interesting and con-tradictory in George Steiner's hermeneutic work on translation theory. Steiner never openly discusses the translator's choice of target language, despite the fact that he repeatedly fails to determine his own native language, suppos-edly possessing equal fluency in English, French, and German. In fact, he even claims that he experiences his first three tongues as perfectly equivalent cen-tres of himself (Steiner 1992:120). Although he does recognise the difficulties in defining the notion of the mother tongue itself, he nevertheless repeatedly indicates that the TL of the translator should also be his mother tongue. For example: "The translator labours to secure a natural habitat for the *alien pres-ence* which he has imported into *his own tongue and natural cultural setting*" (ibid.:365). Or: "He [the translator] will import from abroad conventions, models of sensibility, expressive genres which *his own language and culture* have not yet reached" (ibid.:370). And finally: "[...] it is logically conceivable that the translator, having gained great mastery over a source-language, will con-clude 'I understand this text but find no way of restating it in *my own native tongue*'"(ibid.:372, *emphases are all mine*).

Although he cannot define his native language, and although he has done some translating himself, Steiner never opens the question of choosing one's target language in translation. The principle that the translator is allowed to translate only into his native language seems so deeply rooted in his thought that he never challenges it. He also never disputes another principle, connected to the first one and also typical of the canonised translational norms of the English-speaking world – the principle of fluency and naturalness. This norm has prevailed over other translational strategies in English-speaking cultures and shaped the canon of foreign literatures in English (see Venuti 1995). And since it was also agreed that "perfect" fluency in the TL and the mastery of its different styles could only be achieved in one's mother tongue, the norm that the translator (of at least literary texts) should be a native speaker of the TL became widely accepted too; in fact, it seems even more deeply grounded than the fluency principle.

But norms can change. Thus Lawrence Venuti challenges the absolute validity of the norm of fluency and tries to get his readers to reflect on the ethnocentric violence of a transparent, fluent translation, i.e. of a translation that does not appear to be a translation but imposes itself as the "original" (Venuti 1995: 41) – he even pleads for the production of translations that reveal "the linguistic and cultural difference of foreign texts" (ibid.). But in spite of his openness towards the foreign, and sensitivity to ethnocentric violence, Venuti never touches the problem of the translator's TL, and thus accepts, though perhaps not consciously, the prevailing and ethnocentric norm that proclaims the superiority of TL translators.

Venuti seems to completely ignore the prevailing practice in peripheral language communities, where many translators work into a language that is non-native to them, and the deplorable fact in Western societies that many translations are praised despite the fact that their "translators" did not understand the SL.[9] In fact, he does not find this to be an issue worthy of discussion; thus he quotes Goethe, translated by André Lefevere, a Belgian translating from German into English (ibid.: 99), and he explains the translational practice of Ezra Pound, without mentioning his "Cathay" (1915), despite the fact that this, probably the most praised of Pound's translations of Chinese poems, is also famous for the fact that Pound did not understand Chinese when he translated from E. F. Fenollosa's transcription of and commentary on the ST.

Moreover, his acceptance of the unwritten rule that the translator always works into his/her mother tongue could be seen in his terminology, since he qualifies the language and culture the translator is supposed to translate into as "domestic", and the SL culture as "foreign". For example: "[...] the translator's interpretive choices answer to a *domestic* cultural situation and so always exceed the *foreign* text" (Venuti 1995: 37; *emphasis added*). The same terminology could also be found in his more recent work: "[...] the translator involves the *foreign* text in an asymmetrical act of communication, weighted ideologically towards the translating culture" (Venuti 2000: 484–485; see also

Venuti 1998: 12, 15). According to Venuti then, translators choose a "foreign" text and translate it in conformity with the "domestic" cultural situation, which implies that they never work away from their native language but always into their mother tongue.

Some translation theoreticians, then, accept and generalise the prevailing practice in major-language communities, where, indeed, translation usually takes place into the translator's mother tongue. Thus, for example according to a survey undertaken in *Language Monthly,* the percentage of those translators who translate only into their mother tongue in Britain is as high as 84%, but is much lower in other countries, for example only 35% in Germany (see Beeby 1998: 65) and even lower in other linguistically peripheral countries (for Finland see McAlester 1992). But the generalisation of this practice has some serious consequences: by not taking into account the predominant practice in other linguistic communities, by ignoring the possibility of translations into a non-native language, by undertheorising and uncritically accepting the basic notions of "foreign", "domestic" and "native", these scholars covertly impose yet another ethnocentric norm on the rest of the peripheral world.

Translation into a non-mother tongue and team translation as a part of translation practice

Contrary to common belief, the principle that translation should always be done into one's mother tongue does not have a long history. On the contrary, translation into a non-mother tongue can also be found at the dawn of Western history: in the ancient world, the native language of the translator was not an issue, or at least not one of the criteria according to which the quality of the translation was assessed. Thus, for example, the seventy-two praised translators of the Old Testament from Chaldean into Greek were not all Greek native speakers, which leads to a conclusion that at least some of them were translating out of their mother tongue (Aristeas to Philocrates 1997: 5). While in classical Rome, the great and famous translators were native speakers of Latin, the first Christian Latin translators were Greeks. After a short period when Latin speakers like St. Jerome dominated the field (and Jerome, according to traditional accounts, worked with a group of helpers whom he used as walking dictionaries), we enter a period when nobody translating into Latin spoke it natively. But despite this fact, all the major Greek patristical and philosophical works were translated into Latin by such prominent translators as John Scotus Eriugena, Burgundio of Pisa and Leonardo Bruni (see Kelly

1979:109; Robinson 1997:57). Inverse translation was practised also in the East as well as the West: for example, the first translations of the Buddhist sacred texts from Sanskrit to Chinese were not by Chinese native speakers (see Chu Chi 2000:43–53).

At the end of the Middle Ages, when the most heated debates about translation were usually connected with the translation of the Bible, there were few who found it objectionable that both Reformers and counter-Reformers, such as Erasmus of Rotterdam, translated into Latin. After that period, translation into a non-mother tongue still remained alive in science, where Latin was used as an international *lingua franca* until the end of the eighteenth century.

In the twentieth century, too, translation out of one's mother tongue was not such a rare occurrence: it was and still is a common translation practice in minor-language communities, or to use the current euphemism, in communities which use "a language of restricted distribution or limited diffusion" and which are forced to translate into foreign languages if they want their works to be translated at all (see also McAlester 1992:292–296). The growing interest in this practice and its influence on the theory and didactics of translation and interpreting has also been reflected in two translatological conferences focussing on the topic of directionality: one organised in Ljubljana, the other in Granada (see Grosman et al. 2000; Kelly 2003).

Inverse translation is also common in other large but peripheral language communities, for example in China, where Chinese translators are trying to change, according to them, the distorted image of Chinese poetry created by earlier translations (Lefevere 1995a, b). It seems that this direction of translation is also inevitable for establishing communication between certain immigrant communities and their environment in major-language societies as well. This practice has also triggered a theoretical response – Stuart Campbell in his book *Translation into the Second Language* focuses on the situation in Australia, where certain ethnic communities, such as Arab and Vietnamese, have to rely on Arabic or Vietnamese native speakers to help them communicate in English. Campbell, however, explores inverse translation primarily in an educational environment, and investigates in particular how those non-native speakers, while still acquiring the language, at the same time develop the competence to translate into their second language. He argues that learning to translate is a special form of language learning and that therefore translation into a second language is not deficient *per se* but the product of developing competence (Campbell 1998).

This means that translation into a non-mother tongue is common in small as well as in large language communities; however, it is undoubtedly more common in cultures and communities which do not have a central status and are forced to the global periphery. Very seldom, though, do translators from peripheral cultures work alone – the common practice adopted in those cultures is co-operation between a native and a non-native translator, or a translator who is a native SL speaker and a TL stylist. This practice has also been known in the Western tradition for centuries: thus it is reported that the seventy translators of the *Septuaginta* worked in collaboration "making all details harmonise by mutual comparisons" (Aristeas to Philocrates 1997:5); in the twelfth and thirteenth centuries translators of the Toledo school in Spain often worked in pairs consisting of Muslim and Jewish converts, and seem to have been translating Arabic and Hebrew texts first into one of the vernacular languages and then into Latin (see Beeby 1998:65; Pym 1998:553); and finally, the most frequently translated text in the West, the Bible, is nowadays usually translated in teams. In fact, this co-operation on an equal basis is so frequent that it has a central position in the theory of Bible translation. Thus Eugene A. Nida's *Toward a Science of Translating* is dedicated to such translation teams; in fact, Nida's work goes even further since it is primarily destined to help English-speaking Bible translators (missionaries) who translate the Greek and Hebrew originals into one of the non-Indo-European languages (Nida 1964:147) – i.e. translators who translate from one foreign language into another, often with the help of secondary source languages (French, English), which are used as substitute bases for translation (see also Nida & Taber 1982:6).

At first, Nida insists that ideally the translator should be bilingual in both the source and the target languages, but he soon adds that this ideal is rarely realised (1964:149), and indeed, in case of translators from Classical Greek, bilingualism is unattainable. That is why Nida soon leaves behind the realm of the ideal and focuses on the real problems his group of translator-missionaries faces. Since he is aware of the fact that an ideal set of abilities in one person cannot be found, he distributes the essential elements in the role of translator among several persons in various ways. According to him, in a translation team, roles should be distributed among three persons: one person should interpret the meaning of the source-language message, the second should suggest the equivalent rendering in the receptor language and the third should be responsible for style (ibid.: 153–154).

When Nida describes team translation he has primarily in mind the co-operation between a foreign missionary and a native translator: the missionary being an expert for the languages of the original while the native translator is an expert for the language of the TL culture. Nida insists that all members of such a translation team should know all of the languages involved in the translation, i.e. source and target languages. In case the native translator does not know the language of the original, s/he is not, according to Nida, a translator but merely "an informant or translation helper" (Nida & Taber 1982:102) – which means that, for example, Ezra Pound would not be considered a translator of Chinese poetry but merely a stylistic designer of an already translated text in the target language.

The basic principles of team translation described in Nida's theoretical work could also be applied to the co-operation between translators in peripheral communities, which provides this translational practice with a possible theoretical basis. Translators from peripheral linguistic communities, similarly to Nida's missionaries, work in pairs, but the role of an interpreter of the original text and the role of the translator are combined and done by one person only, usually because the texts they translate do not have a two-thousand-year-long history of exegesis.

Although team translation is often accompanied with mistrust – for example the King of Portugal, Duarte (1391–1438) in *The Loyal Counselor* argues that translation "is best done by one person" (Duarte in Robinson 1997:60) and Samuelsson-Brown claims that translation in pairs "is usually an unsatisfactory compromise" (Samuelsson-Brown 1995:16), inverse and team translation are not only a common fact in the contemporary world but also a theoretically grounded action with fixed rules of conduct.

Translation into a non-mother tongue has thus been known in Western history from Antiquity onwards, and can find one of its possible theoretical groundings in Nida's work. This translational practice is especially common in languages with restricted distribution, in larger linguistic communities which are pushed into a peripheral position because of the global distribution of power and in major-language societies when communicating with ethnic minorities. Western translation theory in general ignores this practice, and accepts the "traditional", i.e. predominantly Romantic, assumption that translators should work only into their own language (when translating all types of text, but especially when translating literature) if they want to create linguistically and culturally acceptable translations. This conviction of the linguistic and cultural inferiority of inverse translations in an opaque way ethnocentrically defends the superiority of post-Romantic West-European concepts concerning translation and translational practice, and thus consequently the *a priori* superiority of the translators and translational practice of major-language communities.

Method and corpus for analysis

To assess whether the assumption of the superiority of direct translation is well grounded or not, a corpus of texts was analysed. The texts chosen for the analysis were originally written in Slovene, a Slavonic language spoken by approximately 2 million speakers in and around the Republic of Slovenia.

Slovenia is bordered by Italy in the west and Austria in the north; to the south, southeast, and east, the republic shares a long border with Croatia, and in the far northeast it touches on Hungary. The country's capital is Ljubljana and it has a population of almost 2 million. For most of its history, Slovenia was divided among the Holy Roman Empire, Venice, Austria, and Hungary; however, the majority of Slovenes were for more than 9 centuries under German rule. During most of the 20th century it was part of Yugoslavia, and in 1991 it became an internationally-recognised independent state.

Language has always been a vital part of Slovene identity and culture. Slovenes were for centuries under different cultural dominations and the only thing that separated them from neighbouring nations was language. Slovene, a South Slavic language written in the Roman (Latin) alphabet, is related to Serbian, Croatian, Macedonian, and Bulgarian, but it also has affinities with West Slavic Czech and Slovak. Although Eastern Slovene dialects are similar to some forms of Croatian, literary Slovene is remote from its Serbo-Croatian counterparts. In addition, there are marked differences among the 46 dialects and standard Slovene, which is derived from two Carniolan speech variants, and which is used in speeches and for writing. Grammatically, Slovene retains certain features not found in any other south Slavic language, such as forms for nouns and verbs expressing the dual number (two persons or things), in addition to singular and plural.

The earliest written record of Slovene is found in the Freising manuscripts, a collection of confessions and sermons dating from around AD 1000. But in spite of this early record, the language was not generally written until the Reformation, when Protestants translated the Bible (1584), wrote tracts in Slovene, and published the first Slovene grammar and dictionary. The next revival of Slovene came at the end of the 18th century, when a Roman Catholic translation of the Bible in Slovene appeared. However, at the beginning of the 19th century, when a large part of the Slovene lands was included in the Illyrian Provinces of Napoleon's French Empire, the French encouraged local initiative and favoured the use of Slovene as an official language. Although many of the changes did not survive the return of Habsburg rule, the period contributed greatly to national self-awareness. Soon after, in 1808, Slovene grammars were published that standardised and codified the language; thus by the mid-19th century, a standard written language was in use. The year 1843 also saw the publication of the first Slovene-language newspaper, followed, at the end of the century, by the formation of the first Slovene political parties. When Austria-Hungary collapsed in 1918, the Kingdom of Serbs, Croats, and Slovenes was formed, later changing its name to Yugoslavia. Here, Slovene autonomy was restricted mainly to cultural affairs, although Slovenes did continue to use Slovene as an official language. After the Second World War, Slovene became one of the three official languages of the Socialist Federal Republic of Yugoslavia, together with Serbo-Croat and Macedonian, and it is now the official language in the Republic of Slovenia (Italian and Hungarian can also be used in areas with Italian and Hungarian national minorities).

The Slovene language proved to be ideal for this study, since it is a typical representative of a minor language or "a language of limited diffusion", whose users have always been forced to translate into foreign languages. The existence of numerous translations by non-native speakers of the TL is thus a common occurence in Slovenia, and allows us to study this phenomenon in a natural environment.

The analysis was applied to literary works, in particular to prose works by Ivan Cankar, the most praised and canonised author in Slovenia, that have been translated into English more than once. The choice of literary works was deliberate: it allowed us to create a corpus of translations where the same text is translated into the same TL by different translators. In Slovenia, and most probably also in other "minor" cultures, non-literary texts only rarely get retranslated; in fact, only the most praised works are considered worthy of retranslation. And since it was believed that a comparison would be more valuable if different translators worked on the same text in a real and not artificially-created situation, Cankar's texts were chosen.

By choosing twentieth-century prose works, an attempt has also been made to create a corpus which bears similarities to other, non-fictional writing. Moreover, following the post-structuralist claim that the traditional boundaries between fictional and non-fictional discourse are blurred, and the argument of some literary theoreticians that "literature" is a functional term and not an ontological one, i.e. "any kind of writing which for some reason or another somebody values highly" (Eagleton 1983:9), which echoes Toury's definition of translations as texts presented or regarded as translations within the target culture (see Toury 1980:37, 43–45; 1985:20; 1995:32), and that all features traditionally applied to literature can be found in non-literary texts and vice-versa, the ambition of this study is that its findings be regarded as valid not only for the texts that traditionally belong to literature but to texts in general.

Since the main aim of the analysis was not only to describe the selected corpus but to determine the effect of the translator's mother tongue on his/her translation, I was selective in the application of existing methods of analysis. Attention was paid primarily to those text levels and relationships that proved to be relevent to the research topic. Thus, first an interpretation of the text is given, followed by a review of the critical response to the particular work. In the presentation of the translation, first the critical response to it (if available) is summarised, then macro-structual characteristics of the translation is described (e.g. introductions, translator's notes, the collection and the publishing house where the translation appeared etc.). Although these data could be used to define the target audience of a particular translation, it should be stressed that the definiton of the target audience and its reception of a particular translation was not the aim of this study, as it focussed primarily on the issue of whether translations into a non-mother tongue manifest any shared characteristics that distinguish them from those carried out into the translator's mother tongue. In fact, a more detailed study of the target audience was abandoned when it was established that the same translator translated for the same journal works by the same author using opposing strategies each time, e.g. once foreignising culturally-specific terms and then domesticating them.

After looking at the macro-structural features of the translation, the text itself is analysed according to the suggestions of Luc van Doorsaer in *Target* in 1995, where he proposed that the original and the translation be read independently, and "potentially relevant passages (from a translational point of view, and based on extra-textual knowledge), as well as distinctive formulations in the ST, are compared with their counterparts in the TT, and vice-versa" (van Doorslaer 1995:265), which means that special attention is paid to shifts in meaning and cultural elements that could represent a problem for a non-native speaker of either the source or the target language.

Those findings are then evaluated by means of a further study involving native speakers of English and their response to the selection of previously-analysed translations. The purpose of this second study is to see if competent native speakers can detect infelicities of style in translations by non-native speakers of the target language. A group of 46 competent native speakers of English from various parts of the English-speaking world were asked to complete a questionnaire that included seven fragments of different English translations of three of Cankar's prose works, indicating whether the translator of a particular passage is, according to their intuitions, a native speaker of English or not.

But before looking at the texts more closely, the mother tongue of the translators involved in the study has to be defined, which in some cases proves to be problematic, as quite a few of them belonged to the Slovene immigrant community in the USA.

Granting the status of a native speaker to immigrants

People who move to a new linguistic environment as adults rarely, if ever, attain the proficiency of a native speaker in the new linguistic community. Some well known exceptions to this rule have already been mentioned, for example Joseph Conrad and Vladimir Nabokov. But it has also been shown that those cases were not complete success stories: Henry Kissinger, for example, immigrated to the USA in his teens, and uses English comparable to that of native speakers but for one detail, he has kept a characteristic, often ridiculed German accent. His brother, who is only a few years younger, has no accent at all (Pinker 1994: 291).

But more than these exceptional cases, average immigrants and their linguistic potentials are much more interesting – and the emergence of linguistic proficiency of the latter were in the focus of attention of F. Grosjean. His research shows that in the United States immigrants often very soon "abandon" their mother tongue and start using English and that this shift from one language to another is usually very rapid (Grosjean 1982: 102). The general language evolution of immigrant families is represented by the following figure:

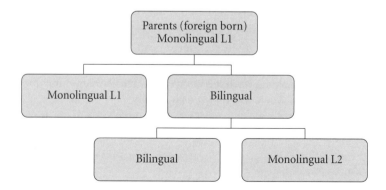

Upon arrival in the United States, the parents are generally monolingual in their mother tongue (L1). They may remain monolingual, for example if they live in a close-knit ethnic minority where they can use their own language at work but also in shops and for conversations with friends. They might also become bilingual in their native language and English (L2), but Grosjean does not here define the level of proficiency in the new language. In fact, most first-generation Americans become bilingual, a few even reject their native language and become monolingual speakers of English (e.g. Russian Jews) (Grosjean 1982: 104).

With their children the language patterns are much more complex:

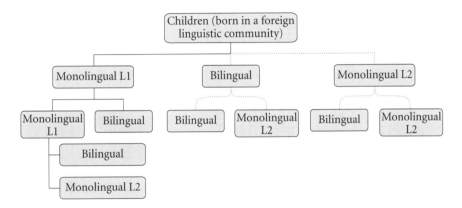

Children born to first generation immigrants in a new linguistic community may become monolingual in the language of the new community, if their parents, in their wish to assimilate as rapidly as possible, do not maintain their mother tongue as well. Some of them are bilingual from the beginning, but most of them follow the route marked with a solid line in the second figure. Thus their early language input will be the native language of their parents (L1), provided that they are the first born and that their parents speak their mother tongue for everyday communication at home. However, quite quickly, English enters the child's life: through the playground, television, peers and above all school. When the child is eight or nine years old, it is usually bilingual in its mother tongue and the language of the new community. After that period some children remain bilingual, others shift entirely to the language of the new linguistic community. The decision between bilingualism and monolingualism depends on various psychosocial factors: if the new environment encourages the use of the language of its parents, if the child lives in a large group where it can use its mother tongue, if religious practice and cultural activism are connected with the language, then there is more chance that the child will remain bilingual. If, on the other hand, the environment is hostile to the foreign language and if the parents are bilingual, the child usually shifts slowly to the new language only (Grosjean 1982: 104–105).

Slovene immigrant community in the USA developed in a similar way to other immigrant communities. While the first generation still kept using the Slovene language, their American-born descendants did not regard competence in the language as a prerequisite for identity as Slovenes, and therefore seldom used their native language. This linguistic shift is described in the *Harvard Encyclopedia of American Ethnic Groups* as follows:

> The immigrant Slovenes attempted to teach the native language to their children, but generally they were not very successful. Without question most second-generation Slovene Americans acquired some familiarity with idiomatic Slovene from their parents, but they did not use it among themselves or when it was not absolutely necessary. Rarely do third- and later-generation Slovenes have any real command of the language.
>
> (Harvard Encyclopedia of American Ethnic Groups 1980: 939)

The second generation of all immigrants is thus at least bilingual, but more often even completely abandons its mother tongue and the language of the environment becomes its first language. However, the question whether the first generation of immigrants may cross over to a new mother tongue remains still open. At what age should a person move to a new linguistic community in order to achieve the level of competence and proficiency in the language comparable to those of native speakers? Linguists are not unanimous on this point: most of them avoid giving an explicit age and suggest that the child should move to a foreign linguistic community before puberty, i.e. before the critical period (and do not define when this critical period is supposed to happen), if it is to achieve proficiency and competence in the language comparable to those of native speakers (e.g. see Davies 1991: 65, 91–92). Some linguists, however, are more precise: for example, Stephen Krashen claims that the critical age is 12 years (Krashen 1981: 76), Steven Pinker sets the critical period to an even earlier period and connects it with maturational changes in the brain (such as the decline in metabolic rate and number of neurons during the early school-age years, and the bottoming out of the number of synapses and metabolic rate around puberty) and therefore sets it around the age of six:

> In sum, acquisition of a normal language is guaranteed for children up to the age of six, is steadily compromised from then until shortly after puberty, and is rare thereafter.
>
> (Pinker 1994: 293)

David Crystal, despite the fact that he insists that people can master a foreign language to levels that are comparable to those achieved by 'natural' bilinguals" (Crystal 1994:368), also claims that the majority of linguistic abilities are developed before the age of five, while some semantic and pragmatic abilities continue to develop during adolescence and even later (Crystal 1994:263).

Linguistics thus does not offer a unique, objectively verifiable answer to the question of what age sets the limit after which one cannot acquire competence and proficiency in the foreign language comparable to those of native speakers. The age limit seems to be fuzzy, but for the purposes of our study it still had to be defined, since some of the translators analysed in the corpus belonged to the first or the second generation of Slovene immigrants to the USA. One of the translators was born in the USA, all the others moved to the new country after the age of 14, which is too late to acquire native-speaker competence in the foreign language even for the most liberal scholars. Therefore the following criteria were observed:

1. If the translator was born in an English-speaking country where he also spent the rest of his life, then, he was considered a native speaker of English, even if both of his parents were Slovene.
2. Since there were no translators of Slovene origin who moved to an English-speaking country before the age of 12, i.e. roughly the beginning of puberty, no representative of the first generation of immigrants was given the status of a native speaker of English.
3. If the translator of Slovene origin moved to an English-speaking country after the onset of puberty, he will be considered as a native speaker of Slovene, despite the fact that he might have received his education and spent his life in the foreign linguistic community.

Presentation of the translators analysed in the corpus

The corpus of works analysed consists of short stories and novels that were in quite a few instances translated more than once and by different translators, which provided an interesting basis for comparison. However, finding biographical data about the translators was sometimes hard, in same cases even impossible. The lives of only a few translators, in particular those who were not only translators but also original authors, are recorded in reference books, for example registers of writers and translators of Slovene origin and of foreign translators working in Slovenia. For the others, newspaper articles of the pe-

riod and the archives of different publishing houses were consulted, in some
cases data were obtained through telephone conversations with the translators
and the relatives of the translators in question. Unfortunately, of a couple, especially those who translated at the beginning of the 20th century, all trace is
lost – which confirms that anonymity is a traditional companion of translators
in the West. While the author of the original is always exposed, the authors of
translations are too often pushed to the background, their presence and their
voice in their work effaced.

The corpus of Ivan Cankar's prose works that were translated into English
more than once revealed an unexpected situation: 14 translators published
their translations of Cankar into English, 7 of them worked individually, 8 in
pairs (one of those who first published his translation as the only translator,
later revised his translations with another translator and is therefore included
in both groups). 4 of them translated from their mother tongue into English,
2 from their foreign language into their mother tongue, 1 from one foreign
language to another (the case of a Serb professor of Slavonic languages in the
USA). This situation proves that in minor-language communities translation
into a non-mother tongue is even much more common than direct translation,
even in the case of literary works.

Eight translators worked in four pairs. Out of those four pairs, two pairs
worked from their foreign language into a foreign language (in one case,
the translator was French by origin, in the other Croatian), one pair from
their foreign language into their mother tongue (both translators were native
speakers of English), and the last pair consisted of a Slovene and an English
native speaker, thus working from one's mother tongue to the other's mother
tongue. Since a critical presentation of all translators and their work would
unnecessarily lengthen this study, and since only 9 out of 14 translators were
included in the questionnaire (i.e. translations of 2 native speakers of the SL,
of 2 native speakers of the TL, and of 3 pairs of translators), only those nine
translators and their work will be presented in more detail.

The first of the two Slovene translators is Louis Adamic (1898–1951), born
to Slovene parents in Blato, Austria-Hungary (now in Slovenia). As a young
boy, he was sent to Ljubljana in order to prepare for the Roman Catholic
seminary, but due to his participation in the Yugoslav National Movement,
which fought against the Austro-Hungarian Empire, he was expelled and
eventually decided to go to America. In December 1913, as a youth of fifteen,
he started his career at a Slovene immigrant newspaper in the USA. He joined
the army and became an American citizen in 1917. He then worked as a
journalist and a free-lance writer, creating all of his works, among them several

novels, in English. Moreover, he seemed to have "crossed over" linguistically – in an interview he gave in English to a Slovene literary magazine of the time he claimed that he had completely lost his mother tongue and embraced English as his new language. When he received a Guggenheim reward for his work in 1932, he travelled back to Yugoslavia and harshly criticised the Serbian regime. Not surprisingly, he welcomed the constitution of the new socialist Yugoslavia and propagated its Marxist ideas in America, so that after the Second World War he even became a member of the Yugoslav Academy of Science and Arts. But although an ardent supporter of the new Yugoslavia at first, he soon became critical of some of its methods and thus added to his traditional opponents representatives of the old regime and members of the so-called reactionary forces who immigrated after and during the Second World War to the States, as well as representatives of the new socialist regime. As a tragic result, Adamic was found dead in 1951 at his home in Milford, New Jersey; he was most probably murdered, and the circumstances of his death have never been explained.

The second Slovene translator is another immigrant to the USA. Jože Paternost (1931–) was born in Rašica (Slovenia) and emigrated with his family after the Second World War to the USA at the age of 14. In 1955 he graduated in German and Russian at the University of Ohio, and later on received a PhD in Slavonic languages at the University of Indiana in Bloomington. In 1977 he became full professor of Slavonic languages at the State University of Pennsylvania. He is now retired.

The first English translator is Henry (Harry) Leeming, born in 1920 in Manchester. He graduated in 1949 at the University of Manchester and successfully defended his PhD thesis in Slavonic languages at London University. Henry Leeming was a teacher for 30 years (from 1955 to 1985) at the Slavonic department of London University and a guest lecturer at the universities of Cambridge, Oxford and Canberra. He is a corresponding member of the Slovene Academy of Arts and Sciences and is now retired.

The second English translator is not a typical example of a native speaker. Anthony J. Klančar (1908–1977) is a representative of the second generation of Slovene immigrants to the USA. He was born in Cleveland (USA) to Slovene parents and died in Cambridge, Massachusetts (USA). He graduated in English in the U.S.A. and spent all of his active life in America. As a journalist, also for Slovene immigrant press, he considered his duty to present to the American public the greatest works of Slovene culture.

Out of the three pairs of translators, only one was typical, consisting of a native speaker of the SL and a native speaker of the TL. The native speaker of

Slovene was Elza Jereb (1935–). Although she was born in Moutiers (France), she is a native speaker of Slovene, since it is her first, home and dominant language. She graduated in English and French at the University in Ljubljana, where she later became a teacher at the Department of Romance Languages. She is now retired. Her English collaborator was Alasdair MacKinnon (1934–). He was born in South Wales in a family that originated from Scotland. In 1954 he graduated in English at Cambridge and worked for three years as a teaching assistant for English language at the University of Ljubljana. While working in Slovenia he learned Slovene and collaborated with Slovene native speakers on translations of Slovene prose and poetry into English.

The second pair consists of two native speakers of English. The first is Anthony J. Klančar who asked professor George R. Noyes to stylistically revise his already existing and published translation. George R. Noyes was, according to Klančar, a professor of Slavonic languages in the USA and a great admirer of Cankar's work (Klančar 1938, 129).

The third pair is most unusual, consisting of one native speaker of the TL and a translator who was a native speaker of neither of the languages involved. Agata Zmajić (1878–1944) (born Rainer von Brestovec) was born in Slavonia (Austria-Hungary, now in Croatia), and died in Friesach (Austria). She travelled extensively and spoke many languages. As a young widow of an officer in the Austro-Hungarian army, she was often in financial difficulties and was thus forced to provide some additional income by translating. No-one knows how she got to translating the text from Slovene into English, since Slovene was not her mother tongue. Agata's relatives claim that she spoke Croatian and identified herself as a member of the Croatian nation, and since Slovene and Croatian are more different than, say, Spanish and Italian, it is surprising that she undertook that translation. For her stylistic advisor, M. Peters-Roberts, it was impossible to find any biographical details. The founders of the Society of Slovene Literary Translators claim that Peters-Roberts did not live in Slovenia, which would be plausible, since it seems that this translator worked with Slovene text on this occasion only. Therefore it would be sound to assume that s/he most probably had no knowledge of Slovene and was a native speaker of the TL.

The translators whose translations were used in the questionnaire were thus classified in the following three groups:

1. Native speakers of Slovene, i.e. of the source language:

    – Louis Adamic; he moved to the USA at the age of 15,
    – Elza Jereb; her home, first and dominant language is Slovene,

– Jože Paternost; he moved to the USA at the age of 14.

2. Native speakers of English, i.e. of the target language:

    – Henry Leeming,
    – Anthony J. Klančar, born in the USA and spent the vast majority of his life in an English-speaking community,
    – Alisdair MacKinnon,
    – George R. Noyes,
    – M. Peters-Roberts.

3. Native speakers of some third language, not English or Slovene:

    – Agata Zmajić, a native speaker of Croatian.

While it was not difficult to define the directionality in translations done by individual translators, this task was much more difficult with pairs of translators. The answer to the question of who the real translator was when more than one person was involved in the translation is sometimes hard to find. In the pair consisting of Elza Jereb and Alisdair MacKinnon the actual translator was the native speaker of the SL, Elza Jereb, however, she insists that MacKinnon's role of was not only a stylistic one, that his contribution to the final translation went beyond stylistic changes only and that many translation solutions were the result of collaboration. In the translation pair of Anthony J. Klančar and George R. Noyes the analysis of previous translations by Klančar shows that the translation, the actual transfer from one language to the other, was done by Klančar and that Noyes acted only as a stylistic advisor. In the case of the translation pair consisting of Agata Zmajić and M. Peters-Roberts the most probable translator was Agata Zmajić, who knew the source and the target languages but was not the native speaker of either of them.

Let us look more closely at the author of the original Slovene texts used as the corpus in this study.

Ivan Cankar and his style

The author Ivan Cankar is regarded as one of the most prominent Slovene prose writers. A prolific writer of short stories, articles, and verse, Cankar was also influential in the development of modern satire, symbolic drama, and the psychological novel. While the topics he treated and the ideas he expressed have received different responses over the years – some critics rejecting his writings, claiming that their structure was often too loose, that his works were monotonous and morally questionable, others praising their tendentious nature and seeking political inspiration in his works – all the critics seemed to be unanimous in their assessment of Cankar's style, considering him as one of the most elaborate stylists in Slovene and admiring his rhythmical, subtle, simple yet eloquent and melodious structures (see e.g. Mahnič 1964:67; Zadravec 1976b:67).

The topics he treated were partly influenced by the poverty he experienced in childhood and also later in life. He was born in 1876 in the small Slovene town of Vrhnika, then part of the Austria-Hungarian Empire. His father was an unsuccessful tailor, who went bankrupt, leaving the mother to provide for the family. The family's financial status deteriorated further in 1879 when their house caught fire. But despite their desolate condition, Ivan went to the primary school in his home town where his talent and brightness were soon recognised. Due to his mother's unyielding support and with the help of friends of the family, he and his brother were sent to secondary school in Ljubljana. However, the support of the family was soon withdrawn, leaving Ivan solely dependent on his mother's meagre earnings. Even at this early age he joined various literary societies, where he started publishing his works.

After finishing his schooling in Ljubljana in 1896, he registered at the Polytechnic in Vienna, but soon lost interest in pursuing an academic career. Instead, he joined a Slovene literary club, where he became acquainted with European Naturalism, but also with the latest literary currents of the period: the Decadent movement and Symbolism. Cankar thus began to earn his living by his writings, in which he defended the oppressed and the poor, while making satirical attacks upon those who exploited them.

At home, in Slovene-speaking parts of the Empire, his first collection of poems *Erotika* was unfavourably received in some circles; in fact, almost every copy was bought and burnt by the Catholic bishop Jeglič in the stoves of the bishop's palace in Ljubljana. This act marked the career of the young poet: after that event all of his works were accompanied by opposing reviews, either being hailed as artistic masterpieces or scorned for their apparent immorality (Bernik 1969:13).

From 1899 to 1909 Cankar thus left Slovenia and remained in Vienna, where he became a member of the socialist movement. When the first general elections were held in the Austro-Hungarian Empire under universal and equal suffrage in 1907 he stood as a candidate for the Yugoslav Social Democratic Party in a small Slovene constituency but failed to be elected. Although he received the highest number of votes among the Slovene socialists, the party did not succeed in entering parliament.

The elections, however, brought him closer to his homeland again – thus in 1909 he returned to Ljubljana for good. His association with the Yugoslav Social Democratic Party soon ended because he found its official politics, in particular its plea for the linguistic unity of the Yugoslav nations, unacceptable. Despite this break, he still remained deeply involved in political life. In fact, in 1913 he was briefly imprisoned for his criticism of the Austrian regime and for the promotion of the idea of a new and independent republic of equal nations.

Despite his political convictions, he was enlisted in the Austro-Hungarian army at the beginning of the First World War, but was soon released on grounds of poor health. Although he still lived to see the collapse of the Austro-Hungarian monarchy and the emergence of Yugoslavia, he did not enjoy the new order for long. Not long after, in October 1918, he fell down stairs and died in Ljubljana hospital two months later (Mahnič 1964: 61–69; Leksikon pisaca Jugoslavije 1972: 403–405).

Cankar's work is listed in literary histories under the heading of the Slovene *Moderna*, i.e. the literary period that characterises Slovene literature at the end of the 19th and the beginning of the 20th century. The term *Moderna* was taken from the work of Herman Bahr,[10] who used the word to describe the literary current announcing the end of the old world and the birth of a new humanity freed from all tradition (Bernik 1987: 7; 1993: 14). Following this general definition, the *Moderna* covers a particular period in the history of Slovene literature and not a stylistically-unified literary trend. This stylistic pluralism was the result of the fact that ideological tendencies and literary styles of the end of the 19th century did not enter the Slovene literary world gradually and in the order in which they appeared in the West; rather, they appeared simultaneously, intertwined into one heterogeneous movement (Kos 1987: 146; Bernik 1993: 13).

This diversity of literary trends and their "synchronic expansion" (Bernik 1983a: 156; 1987: 8) could also be found Cankar's works: there are Decadent elements like listlessness, *ennui*, weariness with life and spiritual uneasiness in his early works *Vinjete* and *Erotika* (Bernik 1993: 14–15). Most of his short stories also reveal the strong influence of Russian psychological and ethical realism as found in the works of Gogol, Dostoyevsky and Tolstoy (Ozvald 1920: 47; Kreft 1969: 69–98; see also Verč 1977: 754–758; Zadravec 1989: 403-427), while in some of his works influences of German and Austrian literary works by Nietzsche and Peter Altenberg can be identified (Bernik 1983a: 15, 17). Impressionism, with its realistic depiction of reality and its sensual and subjective attitude toward life, is also expressed in his *Erotika* and *Vienna Evenings* and to some extent in his novel *The Ward of Our Lady of Mercy* (Bernik 1993: 16–18). Symbolism, the first literary trend to develop in Slovenia almost simultaneously with the Western countries (Bernik 1985a: 155; 1988: 168), can be detected in the novel *On the Hillside (Na klancu)* and partly in *The Ward of Our Lady of Mercy*, while the first traces of Expressionism appear in his collection of short stories *Dream Visions* (Bernik 1993: 21–23).

Although Cankar's work does vary and show influences of Decadence, Realism, Impressionism, Symbolism and Expressionism, the common denominator for all these heterogeneous literary currents remained his style of writing. Indeed, some scholars claim that the only thing the authors of *Moderna* had in common was a particular style and the rhythm permeating their works (see Pogorelec 1969). Cankar, for example, admitted that if having to choose between grammatical correctness and stylistic clarity and beauty, he would immediately opt for grammatical irregularity (letter to H. Tuma, 29 March 1918 (Cankar 1976: 65)) and choose words according to the rhythm they created. In the same letter he continues: "1. The rhythm in style is more important than grammar. 2. Rhythm depends on the meaning. 3. The word depends on the rhythm. 4. A pure harmony between consonants and vowels is essential" (Cankar 1976: 65).

This "spoiled and elaborate style" (Cankar 1972: 98), as he himself called it, was often meticulously analysed by various Slovene scholars, who focused on his use of rich metaphors (Mahnič 1956/57: 98–100), puns, personification, irony, sarcasm and paradox. It shows traces of two important stylistic models: Slovene folk literature (Breznik 1935: 508) and the language of the Bible (Bele 1909: 349–374; Mahnič 1956/57: 102–104; Pogorelec 1977: 299; Bernik 1985a: 169; 1993: 22). And indeed, in most of his works Cankar refers to Biblical parables, his works contain almost literal quotations from the Bible and his style is profoundly influenced by Biblical parallelism, in particular his novel *Yerney's Justice* (Bele 1909: 349–347; Mahnič 1956/57: 104; Cvetek-Russi 1977: 753).

By using marked syntactical structures with frequent inversions, he creates a specific rhythmical and melodious style (see Mahnič 1956/57: 152–153). This rhythm becomes in some of his works so regular that certain scholars have even detected a dactilo-rhythmical foundation (Sovré 1956/57: 326–327). Formal address and rhetorical questions are also quite frequent. His sentences are long, usually consisting of three subordinate clauses, with alternating asyndeton and polysyndeton. In addition, numerous figures of speech are employed:

- iteration: "Black mud on the roads, black dust on the field, on the villages; black were the waters, black was the sky" (*Kurent* Cankar 1973:74).
- anaphora and epiphora: "They are lost, they are dead; in vain were all the tears, in vain you went blind, in vain your hands started prematurely to shake…" (*Na klancu* Cankar 1971). "Whatever happened to me, merry or sad, for me that was like a song; a friendly nod, a kind glance, for me that was like a song; also the pain, also that was a song, a particularly sweet one" (*Dream Visions* Cankar 1975:63).
- anadiplosis: "When the door silently closes after life, the conscience delivers its just and inexorable sentence; and that sentence is clearly written on the forehead, cheeks and lips." (*Her Image* Cankar 1974:235)
- refrain: "We had no doubt. It was getting dark and in the evening dinner must be served. Hard and horrible is the child in his trust. Mother, in the evening dinner must be served; go and get it, dig it out of the earth, tear it from the clouds!" (*Holy Communion* Cankar 1974:239)
- parallelism, typical of Hebrew poetry: "I know you, little sister. I know exactly why you are so quiet. Your thought is a mortal sin which will never be taken away! I know you, little brother, I know exactly your silent reproach against me! Your sin, as well, will never be taken away!" (*Holy Communion* Cankar 1974:241)

The genre most frequently used by Ivan Cankar was the sketch – a specific form of short story, typical of Slovene literature of the period. This brief fictional prose narrative developed with the emergence of contemporary journalism in Slovenia at the end of the 19th century, enabling Slovene writers to publish their works in feuilletons. The sketch is always very short, depicting a single event or an emotional state. It is usually written in the first person, and is often accompanied with a more abstract reflection at the beginning and the end (Kos 1983:12; 1987:175–176; Zadravec 1982:77).

Most of the works translated into English are sketches which, despite their limited length, nevertheless reveal the stylistic richness of Cankar's longer works. And this elaborate style caused most of the problems for translators, who almost unanimously decided for the symbolic and expressionist part of his writings.

Analysis of the texts
Presentation of the selected originals

Nineteen prose texts by Ivan Cankar have been translated into English more than once, and all of them have been analysed. Although some of them might be referred to later on, a full report on the analysis seemed unnecessary. The following chapter will focus on the presentation of only those three texts whose translations were included in the questionnaire that will be discussed later, enabling us thus to interpret the results more accurately.

The Ward of Our Lady of Mercy

The Ward of Our Lady of Mercy was written between 1902 and 1903, and published in the spring of 1904. The structure of the work, consisting of a sequence of individual units, was regarded as innovative at the time of publication. The content of the work also proved to be shocking and scandalous to the original audience – it discussed themes the contemporary public did not want to hear. The ward of the title is in a hospital for incurably sick children in a large and unnamed city, where fourteen girls are dying, most probably of syphilis, passed on by their parents. The main character, Malchie, is the only girl who is aware of the fact that they have been put into hospital to die. Despite this awareness, she has no wish to return home, since she finds death her friend and neighbour. Her companions are portrayed as individuals and come from all levels of society: Lois, like Malchie, does not want to return to her rich artistocrat home and to her adulterous mother and drunken father. Katie and Tina come from a working-class family; Katie's body is covered with sores and she speaks to no-one, while fourteen-year-old Tina would like to leave: she is tormented by her awakening sexuality, but is doomed to early death like all the others. Pauline, a Jewish girl, is lonely and proud, while Rezika is kind and generous. Then there is Minka, the hunchback Brigid, and a blind girl, Toni, always yearning for the sun. Toni is the only one to return home, to an outside world plunged into corruption and misery. She is forced to leave the serenity of the ward and return to her dissolute father and adulterous step-mother whose perverted daughter sexually abuses the blind girl. The novel ends with the death of Malchie, symbolically represented as a mystical union with Christ.

The central themes of the novel are religion and death, but also disease, alcoholism, puberty and the erotic, also in its deviant, paedophile forms. Literary critics thus found in it a characteristic display of naturalistic motifs which Cankar tried to remodel according to the precepts of symbolistic narrative techniques (Kos 1976: 24; Bernik 1985: 166). *The Ward* is nowadays seen as one of the few Slovene European novels (Kos 1976: 31), and it is therefore surprising that it has been translated into English only twice.[11]

The novel allows for different and opposing interpretations. Thus soon after its publication the darkest aspects of the novel, describing the physically and socially-scarred girls, provoked extremely negative reviews, from both sides: liberal and conservative. The most praised liberal critic of the time, Fran Kobal, describes the work as "refined pornography, brought to artistic perfection" (Kobal 1904), and the conservative, right-wing journal *Dom in svet* rejected the work completely as immoral (D. S. 1904: 308). Cvetko Golar in *Slovan* (Golar 1903/1904: 187–188), a central-left literary magazine, attempted to be appreciative of the work, but could not avoid emphasising the feeling of "repulsion" one gets when reading the work – which did not help to promote a different understanding of the text. On the other hand, the critic Pavel Mihalek in the publication of Social Democrats *Naši zapiski,* was enthusiastic (Mihalek 1903/1904: 95), and so was Ivan Merhar who wrote in the most prominent liberal literary journal of the time, *Ljubljanski zvon,* that "from behind the darkness and shadows there appears a ray of hope, although weak and dimmed, but nevertheless an encouraging ray of hope and change for the better" (Merhar 1904: 380). Cankar's cousin, Izidor, who was a renowed literary critic and art historian and also one of the few who was capable of seeing beyond the mere surface, wrote: "The book starts with a poem of yearning and ends with a poem of saved souls. . ." (Iz. Cankar 1927: 12).

Literary criticism after the Second World War no longer regarded the naturalistic elements of *The Ward* as unacceptable; the most prominent literary critic in the sixties thus read the novel as the work in which Cankar, through the use of Christian motifs and symbolism, elevates the suffering child to the level where she becomes a sacrificial lamb and the saviour of straying humanity (Slodnjak 1967: 184). Within this horizon of understanding, the death of one of the main characters, Malchie, becomes the meaningful climax of existence, the entrance into a new and true life, individual salvation and ascension, the first and the last erotic encounter consummated in mystical union with Christ (see Slodnjak 1969: 186–187). Such a reading seems to be also, according to his cousin Izidor, close to the interpretation of the text by its author:

> Regarding the criticism of my work, let me tell you this: one of my works was understood in a completely wrong and twisted manner. That was *The Ward of Our Lady of Mercy*. My thought was as pure as spring water when I wrote it. That is why the critical responses made me angry, although only great literary scandals make me feel that way. The idea of *The Ward* is not filthy, but tragic: fourteen sick girls anticipating life and health in death.(Iz. Cankar 1960: 9–10)

More contemporary literary criticism has focussed on the specific form and structure of the work: some defining it as a collection of short stories (Bernik 1983b: 164, 483), others as a cyclical, impressionistic novel (Kos 1976: 15–24, 1984: 88, 1987: 169). Naturalistic motifs, numerous Decadent elements and an Impressionistic style are emphasised in the work (Kos 1984: 88, 1987: 165; Bernik 1987: 14). The text reveals to some critics the author's struggle with sexuality (Kermauner 1974: 105; cf. Kos 1996) and the final goal of the protagonists is no longer seen in a mystical marriage but in a sensual and emotional fulfilment hidden in death (Kos 1976: 53–59).

A Cup of Coffee

At the beginning of 1914 Ivan Cankar prepared a collection of short stories with the title *My Field* (*Moja njiva*), but he died before it appeared. Some of the short stories destined to appear in that collection were published two years later in the book *My Life* (1920); however, not all of the stories were included in the selection and the original distribution of the texts was changed (see Koblar 1920: 139). It was as late as 1935 that the book appeared as it was originally intended, i.e. divided into four major parts, each bearing its own title. The short story *A Cup of Coffee* was published in the last part, entitled *By the Holy Grave* (*Ob svetem grobu*).

At the time of its first appearance, *My Field* did not arouse any adverse reactions among the critics – everyone seemed to have liked it. Thus, for example, France Vodnik in the conservative *Dom in svet* only mentions that the book was published and that the values expressed in it are commendable (Vodnik 1935b: 445). A more detailed, but also appreciative review was published in the liberal *Ljubljanski zvon*, where *My Field* was described as one of the most beautiful books by Cankar and "the most brilliant proof of his artistic growth" (Gspan 1936: 98–102).

Contemporary Slovene literary history places *My Field* in the Symbolist literary current on the basis of its themes and in Expressionism with regard to the formal and stylistic features of the sketches (Zadravec 1982: 88; Kos 1987: 177); and indeed, the sketches are filled with lyrical reasoning, Decadent and Romantic features are replaced by Symbolist and Expressionist elements, while the style is more abstract (see Kos 1987: 177).

The last section of *My Field* consists of 11 sketches entitled *By the Holy Grave*, all of them dedicated to the memory of a mother. Cankar's treatment of the relationship between a son and his mother seemed to many readers and also to his English translators as the most characteristic aspect of Cankar's creativity – as many as 10 out of the 14 translators treated in this study translated at least one of the sketches from that section. And this representativeness is reflected in the fact that Cankar's understanding of the relationship between a mother and her son, as well as the significance and importance of the mother in his writings, have often been critically discussed (see e.g. Puhar 1982: 25–29).

In most of the sketches included in *By the Holy Grave* the mother is represented as a caretaker and guardian of her children, as a dying or even dead mother and as a spiritual consort who can, even after her own death, console her son in his moments of crisis. Almost all of the sketches describe the relationship between the sacrificing, loving mother on the one hand and the ungrateful and wrongful son on the other. This relationship results in the emergence of the son's burning feelings of guilt, intensified by the fact that while his mother was alive they had not shared the same worldview. But when remembering his mother, the narrator finds strength in her expressed religious feelings which eventually helps him to overcome his own crisis (Bernik 1976a: 80, 1983a: 277, 1983b: 443, 1987: 243). The themes of sin, repentance, penitence and salvation intertwine in these eleven sketches and reveal a typical Catholic but also individualised moralism (Kos 1987: 179) – and this similarity between Cankar's treatments of the filial relationship to the mother with the Catholic cult of the Virgin Mary proved problematic for many scholars.

For some interpreters of his work, Cankar's mother thus became "the supreme ethical principle and the symbol of a covenant and debt" (Pirjevec 1964: 436), the only unchangeable and stable principle to whom everything else has to adapt to in order to become real and true (Pirjevec 1964: 19). The mother becomes a symbol, larger than life, bestowing the meaning of life to her son (Pirjevec 1964: 437) and revealing to him that he is a "free historical subject who exists, who is and is not nothing".

Not only Pirjevec, but numerous other scholars interpret this relationship according to their own understanding of the world; for example, quite a few of them attempt to parallel this fictional relationship between the mother and her son to the real relationship between Cankar and his mother. The narrator is simply identified with Cankar and the mother with Cankar's mother (see e.g. Vidmar 1971; Bernik 1976a: 82, 1983b: 430, see also 1983a: 227, 1983b: 490). Cankar was aware of this possible reading of his works at the time of their publication and therefore insisted that no simplistic conclusions be drawn:

> I would like to add that all those merry and sad stories were not written by me, i.e. the person who now talks to you and loves you from all his heart; they were written by someone you do not know and never will. Divide your respect if you have any: bestow the better part to me, to the one who walks with you, and give the rest to the one who writes stories and remains unknown.
>
> (Cankar 1959a: 294)

Although Cankar undoubtedly created all of his works out of his own experience, his writings should nevertheless be critically appraised in their totality; in fact, it would be very difficult to pinpoint the character in his works who undoubtedly and professedly expresses the author's point of view. Cankar is never only the doubting son but also the religious mother, they both stem from him and are the fruit of his creativity; he is not only the one who doubts and suffers torture, but also the one who suffers and saves; and finally, Cankar is not only an internalised dichotomy of doubt and faith but the one "you do not know and you never will", who partly and evasively reveals and hides himself in a complex, contradictory and illusive text.

If not simplistically identified with Cankar's mother, then the mother in these sketches is seen as a symbol larger than life: thus Izidor Cankar writes that in Cankar's works the maternal figure blends with the face of Virgin Mary, becoming "something transcending humanity, something that is eternal, miraculous and immaculately sacred" (Iz. Cankar 1969: 349). The most prominent post-war critics, Bernik and Vidmar, also argue that the image of the mother in the sketches surpasses mere descriptions of a pure, self-sacrificing and suffering woman and that the author sacralised her, making her "a martyr saint" (Cankar 1974: Her Grave: 279). Her grave thus becomes the Holy Grave, her letter Holy Scripture, her memory the holy memory, her sacrifice for her family the Holy Communion for her children, and visits to her grave a holy pilgrimage (Bernik 1976a: 80, 1983a: 277, 1983b: 430–431; Vidmar 1977: 9). While Bernik and Kos argue that Cankar's symbolic use of Christian religious vocabulary is an original artistic reworking of the Catholic liturgy and religious symbols (Bernik 1983a: 277, 1983b: 431, 1987: 219; Kos 1987: 177), others claim that Cankar's cult of the mother is a natural continuation of the Marian cult in Slovenia (Vodušek in Vodnik 1935a: 110).

It seems that at the end of the day the understanding of the concept of the mother in Cankar's work usually corresponds to the interpreter's relationship towards Christianity. Thus for example, Lacanian scholars see in Cankar's mother the bearer of the phallus, the signifier or the herald of a symbolic castration (Močnik 1971: 88[31]; Žižek 1978: 206). The son is incessantly tormented by guilt and suffocated by the obvious suffering of his mother.

> To put it simply: all of Cankar's unending litanies about his mother only hide and with that symptomatically reveal the fact of immense relief that he was freed from his mother; they are a kind of neurotic conjuring directed at keeping his mother away, wishing that she would never return.   (Žižek 1978: 206)

A similarly negative attitude is developed by Heideggerean critics who claim that the mother is not the one who possesses the phallus (Hribar 1983: 45) but the one who acts in the name of the Other as the Almighty (Hribar 1983: 45[16]), and thus remains a "bad" influence in her son's life:

> Cankar's mother is a bad mother, because she is too good. With her whining goodness and piousness she managed to annihilate (also in the name of God the Father, the Other as the Almighty) the ideal image of the humiliated real father, whose humiliation was due to biological and social reasons. She thus managed to create in critical situations an unknown horror instead of trust, and this horror then followed Cankar throughout his life.   (Hribar 1983: 48)

And indeed, the mother's suffering causes suffering and a sense of sin in her son. But while suffering seems "bad" for Slovene Heideggerians, in Cankar's horizon of understanding, which is often close to that of traditional Christianity, suffering becomes redemptive since it leads beyond life.

Despite different interpretations of Cankar's conceptualisation of the mother, it is obvious that she and the relationship of her children towards her occupy a central and essential position in Cankar's work. This claim also seems to be substantiated by the fact that these sketches are the works of Cankar most often translated into English, which means that for their translators they best represent Cankar's work as a whole.

The sketch *A Cup of Coffee,* first published in the liberal literary magazine *Ljubljanski zvon* in 1910, discusses the concept of sin, which is considered not so much as the violation of a general moral principle, but more trespassing against internal commandments of the heart (see Bernik 1983b: 429). The sketch opens with an abstract reflection on how a sin, although it might appear minute to others, can oppress the soul indefinitely, and how the grievousness of the sin is always judged by the individual and never by the state or the church. A short story then follows where a son, a writer, tells his mother that he would like a cup of coffee, although he is aware that his mother does not even have the money to buy bread for the family. The mother nevertheless manages to bring him a cup, but the son, completely immersed in his work, in a moment of distraction, tells her to go away. He is immediately aware of his cruelty and tries to make things right again, but it is too late – the sin carves itself into his soul for ever.

The sketch has been translated into English five times, but the translations, with the exception of Adamic's version, have received almost no critical response.

Children and Old People

This sketch was published in a collection of short stories entitled *Dream Visions* (*Podobe iz sanj*) that appeared during the First World War, in December 1917, in Ljubljana. Most of the sketches first appeared in the "conservative" literary journal *Dom in svet* in the period between 1915 and 1917, i.e. during the war and at a time when the magazine was edited by Cankar's cousin Izidor Cankar.

In *Dream Visions* problems of the First World War period are approached, the sketches become even shorter and quite a number of them no longer depict an event but offer a reflection, a symbolic meditation, dream or grotesque (Cankar 1975: 289–290; Bernik 1983a: 278, 1983b: 474; Kos 1987: 177; Zadravec 1991: 187). They are thus usually classified in two larger units: the first group consisting of more or less traditional, i.e. realistic sketches – like for example the sketch *Children and Old People*; the second group consisting of symbolic, expressionist sketches depicting almost no events and no realistic characters (see Bernik 1983b: 473). The translators into English almost unanimously decided for the first group of sketches, i.e. the traditional, realistic ones.

The collection is Cankar's last work and the only one he published during the First World War. In it, he expresses the wish to feel close to another human being, to his suffering, fear and horror, while exploring the human desire to find again its soul. Besides the obvious use of the expressionist idea of brotherhood among men (see Bernik 1981: 124, 1983a: 277), Cankar openly uses traditionally Christian notions. The narrator thus defines the three greatest values in his life: Mother – Homeland – God, as the only trinity that defends him from Death (Bernik 1981: 129, 1983b: 470, 1987: 226–227).

And this explicitly expressed religious elation, this optimism grown out of the painful experience of the horrors of the war, proved to be the most exciting to his critics.

Dream Visions and *The Cross on the Hill* were Cankar's only works that were well received by the critics and a wider readership. The immediate response to this work was unanimously positive – in Slovenia as well as in Croatia. In contrast to his other works, this time the Catholic critics wrote the most appreciative reviews, while the liberal critics showed some reservations. In fact, some of the critics were even euphoric, thus in the journal *Jugoslovan* we read: "For his great love for humanity Ivan Cankar will receive gratitude from his mother and his homeland, and God will repay him" (Mazovec 1917: 3). Cankar was not happy with such eulogies – but despite his protests, the collection was continuously showered with praise. *Slovenski narod* thus describes the collection as "a work of beautiful poetry, of pure, even purest lyricism" (Ilešič 1917: 2). The liberal *Ljubljanski zvon* finds in Cankar's depiction of human helplessness the rejection of resignation and the light of optimism (Glonar 1918: 147). And this optimism was detected by most of the critics in Cankar's expressed religiousness: thus some of them claim that the sketches "breathe in the framework of poetry and religousness" (Gangl 1918: 5), that the collection is a book of "goodness, love and faith" (Albrecht 1918: 192), some critics even go so far as to recommend the work for reading during Lent (Debevec 1918: 1–2) and argue that *Dream Visions* contain not only religious elements, but that with them the renegade Cankar finally returned to a religious understanding of the world (Pregelj 1917/18: 80–85). The response in the Social-Democratic camp was therefore reserved – they felt as if Cankar had changed sides and somehow joined the conservatives (see e.g. Kristan 1918: 1). Since Cankar was mainly praised as a Social Democrat and his expressed religiousness was suppressed after the Second World War, the book had a similarly reserved reception in the Socialist period.

At the time of its first publication, the book was well received in Croatia, despite the language barrier. The collection was hailed as the peak of Slovene, or even world literature (Lah 1918: 271–277; Sokačić 1918: 428–430); the book was appreciated by the public and sold so well that it was reprinted in 1920.

The sketch *Children and Old People* was thus first published in 1916 in the journal *Dom in svet* and then a year later in the collection *Dream Visions*. The sketch in a realistic manner depicts how children accept the news that their father "fell in Italy". The four children cannot understand the consequences of this news and stare "into something unknown, incomprehensible to the heart and the mind" (Cankar 1975: 23). While the wife of the deceased cries in the stable, his parents, like his children, embrace the pain in silence.

This sketch is one of the most frequently translated sketches into English; in fact, it has been translated six times. Unfortunately, of some of the early translators all trace is lost.

Analysis of the texts
Presentation of the selected translations

Let us now look at the seven translations of the above-presented texts more closely. After briefly reviewing the critical response to the translations (if available), and describing some of the macro-structural characteristics of the texts, special attention is paid to shifts in meaning, stylistic features and cultural elements that could represent a problem for a non-native speaker of either the source or the target language.

The Ward of Our Lady of Mercy by Henry Leeming

The Ward of Our Lady of Mercy was translated into English by Henry Leeming in 1968, but was published as late as 1976 in Ljubljana by the state-funded publishing house Državna založba Slovenije. The translation is not accompanied by notes or a glossary, but with a five-page introduction where Anton Slodnjak briefly presents the life of Ivan Cankar and draws parallels between the topics treated in the novel and the fate of Malchie (short for Amalia), one of the daughters of Albina Löffler, a divorced dress-maker and Cankar's landlady in Vienna. Malchie Löffler contracted tuberculosis of the bone and (like her namesake in *The Ward*) died in a hospital two years before the publication of the novel. Slodnjak's introduction also attempts to find in Cankar's work the influences of different European literary currents of the period and compares his work to that of Goethe, Victor Hugo, Dostoyevsky and Hauptmann.

But even more interesting than the introduction are the two notes following it. The first one quotes Alfred Löffler, saying that his sister Malchie fell when she was a small child, contracted an incurable disease from that fall and never recovered after that. Alfred is also quoted as saying that their tenant Ivan Cankar was very fond of her. This note adds the text an apparently close connection with factual events taken from Cankar's biography, which was typical of positivist post-war literary criticism. In the second note, the reader is informed that the work was rejected at the time of its appearance and that the public was particularly scandalised by Chapters 6 and 8, which were seen as refined pornography, brought to artistic perfection. In Chapter 6 Cankar describes the earlier history of Lois and Brigid, the life of Lois's adulterous mother and father and of Brigid's prostituting mother, in Chapter 8 he depicts the sexual abuse of blind Toni. It continues by quoting Cankar's reply that the work is "as pure as spring water", adding that the author forbade the translation of Chapter 8, depicting the life of Toni before entering the hospital, in the Russian and Czech version.[12] Thus although the English translation does include the "problematic" chapters, the reader nevertheless gets cautioned about them.

The translation by Henry Leeming reveals shifts at different levels: from changes of punctuation, distribution of the text in paragraphs, omissions and extensions, to changes of meaning. For example, Leeming consistently shortens Cankar's paragraphs and sentences and thus also changes the author's characteristic style, which creates a specific rhythmical effect in the original with the use of two or three subordinate clauses or two or three phrases within a sentence (Mahnič 1956/57; Pogorelec 1969, 1976/77, 1977). Leeming is consistent in his changes, which results in the English text being expressed in a more abrupt, jerky style. Shortening of the sentences also entailed extensive changes of punctuation: commas and semicolons are replaced by full stops.

With regard to changes of meaning, some of the shifts are less radical than others, since they do not affect the meaning of the whole sentence or paragraph, and therefore are unlikely to change the understanding of the novel itself:

(1)   Stale so ob postelji in so molčale, zunaj pa se je že nagibal dan, že so plavale sence na nebu, plezale so že tam zunaj po *zidu gor*[13] ... (Cankar 1972:22)

Leeming: They said nothing but remained at her bedside while outside the sun sank in the west till dark shadows lay across the sky and far away in the distance crept along the *mountain wall* ... (Cankar 1976:33)

Leeming translates "plezale so že tam zunaj po zidu gor" (LT[14]: "crept along the wall") with "and far away in the distance crept along the mountain wall"; the wall of the hospital thus becomes a mountain wall. Instead of a dreary view of a wall offered by a hospital window, the translation grants a view of the natural world and thus adds a new dimension to the life of the sick girls. This shift might suggest that the hospital is situated outside the city, or at least somewhere where children can enjoy natural beauty and thus diminishes the expectations of the girls waiting for the promised trip to nature – the Garden of Eden.

However, other elements depicting the surrounding city are so strong that despite this change the translation still seems to convey the stiffling atmosphere of a large city.

Similarly, he changes the meaning in the next example:

(2) Komaj toliko so bile odprte trepalnice, da se ji je samo pisano bleščalo skozi senco dolgih temnih *vejic*. Odprle so se duri; prišel je v sobo angel, zeleno drevesce je imel v roki. (Cankar 1972:79)

Leeming: Her eyelids were almost closed but a bright glimmer of light shone through the shadows of the long dark *branches* outside. The door opened and an angel came into the room carrying a small green tree in his hand. (Cankar 1976:104)

In this case Leeming depicts the hospital as being surrounded by trees and dark branches. In the original the greenery is not mentioned at all, the noun "vejice" means "eyelashes" in this case, although it can also mean "branches" in other contexts. Both those examples reveal that Leeming might have misunderstood the original, being a non-native speaker of Slovene. There are more examples revealing his less than full mastery of the source language:

(3) Prestrašila se je, kadar se je bližal korak, *zakaj* vsi ljudje so bili zli … (Cankar 1972:51)

Leeming: She was terrified at the sound of footsteps. *Why* were all the people so bad? (Cankar 1976:69)

In this case the conjunction "zakaj" which in the contemporary Slovene is almost always used as a relative or interrogative pronoun corresponding to the English 'why' is used as a causative conjuction which could be translated with "because" or "since". It is obvious that the translator did not recognise this slightly archaic use of the word. He also misunderstood the following literary use of the word "ali":

(4) "Zakaj nečeš domov?" je vprašala Brigita.
        Lojzka se je komaj ozrla in ni odgovorila.
        Ali Brigita bi bila šla s tako bogatim gospodom, s tako elegantno damo na bogat dom, v veliko hišo, kjer je vseh sladkosti dovolj. Zakaj tudi Brigita je nagnila glavo in je poslušala, kadar je šlo življenje mimo, zdrznila se je in bi ubogala, kadar je šla zunaj mimo okna starka in je vabila … (Cankar 1972:67)

> Leeming: "Why don't you want to go home?" asked Brigid.
>   Lois just looked round at her but made no answer. *Would* Brigid have gone off with such a grand lady to that rich home, that great house with all good things in plenty? Certainly, Brigid, like Tina, bowed her head and gave ear as life passed by, shuddered and would have done anything she was told when the old woman outside the window beckoned … (Cankar 1976:89)

Although the use of the word "ali" meaning 'but', 'however' is literal and rarely used, it is clear that Cankar used it in this sense. The translator again took the most common meaning of the word, usually translated by 'why' or just indicating a yes/no question and translated it accordingly with "would" as part of a question.

Some of the changes, however, cannot be explained by the fact that he might have misunderstood the original wording:

(5)   Daj ga iz roke, Malči, *poginil bo*! (Cankar 1972:38)

Leeming: Put him down, Malchie, or *he'll fly away*! (Cankar 1976:52)

The girls get a canary in their room and are jealous of Malchie when she caresses it – at the same time this sentence forbodes its death; the canary dies of fear when one of the visitors tries to catch it and hold it in his hands. The wording "poginil bo" does not have a double meaning in Slovene and bears no phonological similarity to Slovene equivalent of "he'll fly away" – "odletel bo". Leeming here chose to translate the original wording "poginil bo" (LT: "he'll die") with "he'll fly away", thus changing death into flight and does not convey the foreboding.

In the next example, although marginal at first sight, Leeming changes the meaning of the story and influences our perception of the social background of the main character:

(6)   /.../ in kadar je šla z doma in jo je spremljal mladi gospod, je imela na glavi klobuk z rožami in svilenimi trakovi, na rokah rokavice, *pozlačen braslet za pestjo*. (Cankar 1972:71)

Leeming: /.../ and when she went in the young man's company she wore a hat with flowers and silk ribbons, gloves on her hands and a *gold bracelet* on her wrist. (Cankar 1976:94)

In this description of Malchie's mother Leeming translated the adjective "pozlačen" (LT: "gilded") with "gold", which might give the reader the false impression that Malchie lived in a relatively well-off environment. Descriptions of the world outside the hospital are rare in the original, the reader only gets a glimpse into the social reality the sick girls came from, so that such details are important. Malchie has a working-class background, her mother does not own gold but only gilded jewellery. By giving her a gold bracelet, she climbs up the social ladder. This change might have been again the result of the fact that Leeming is not a native speaker of Slovene and might have misunderstood the word. On the other hand, this change might have been the result of his negligent reading of the original, like the following one:

(7)   "Rezika, – *mati*!" (Cankar 1972:23)

Leeming: "Rezika – your *father*'s here!" (Cankar 1976:33)

In this case Leeming translated "mati" (LT: "mother") with "father". Rezika, one of the sick girls in the hospital, is frightened of her mother and loves her father. Lois, who likes teasing, calls out this sentence in order to frighten Rezika. Rezika turns pale and hides herself under the blanket, but her fear immediately turns into joy when she sees her father. When Leeming changes "mother" into "father", the reader does not know why Rezika is first in a panic and then relieved when her father appears.

The next translation shift also changes our reading of the text:

(8)   "Potrpi, Tina, ozdraviš in *pojdeš*." (Cankar 1972:54)

Leeming: "Be patient, Tina. You'll soon get better. Then *you'll go home again.*" (Cankar 1976:73)

Tina is the most mature girl in the hospital. In contrast to the others, she wants a life outside hospital walls, she longs for love and romantic encounters. But going out does not mean going home for her. In fact, going home would be the worse of her nightmares: before being hospitalized, she was exposed by her family on a heap of dung in the middle of winter. Malchie sees Tina's suffering and tries to console her by saying to her that she shall leave the hospital and enter the world she desires. When instead of "pojdeš" (LT: "you shall leave"), Leeming uses "you'll go home again", in his translation Malchie's benevolent words change into a threat which does not correspond to the feeling of friendship the two girls share.

In *The Ward of Our Lady of Mercy* Cankar often uses the symbolism of place and creates a parallelism of different worlds. The incurably sick girls know three worlds: the first is the corrupt and cruel world of the city surrounding the hospital. For the girls the city and its inhabitants personify the horror that bursts into their world during visiting hours and even kills their beloved canary. The second world is that of the hospital – a world that already touches on the new, real life, but is still dangerously close to the world surrounding the hospital. Thus the world of the hospital can lead to the third, real life, hidden in death, or to the spiritual death praised by the life outside the hospital walls. The third world, anxiously anticipated by most of the girls, is the everlasting, heavenly life after death – this is the place Malchie enters in the closing sentences of the novel.

Leeming in his translation often distorts the symbolic distinction between the corrupt world outside the hospital, the paradisial life after death and the warmth of the hospital ward:

> (9)   ... od daleč še je prihajal moten, nerazločen šum – šum mesta, ki je živelo *tam daleč, daleč onkraj življenja* ... (Cankar 1972:25)
>
> Leeming: From somewhere far away there still came a dull, confused noise – the noise of the town, which had its own being out there in the distance, somewhere *where life still held sway* ... (Cankar 1976:36)

For the girls in the hospital, the real life is the life after death – their previous life in the city full of suffering represents not life, but death, the death of the soul. This often repeated paradox is lost in the translation, where Leeming's translation of "šum mesta, ki je živelo tam daleč, daleč onkraj življenja" (LT: "the noise of the city which had lead its life far away, far beyond life ...") gives the impression that the girls thought that real life was the life of the city.

The hospital in the original represents a kind of waiting room with a door/death leading to the new and eternal life.

> (10)   Videle so tudi brezštevilne luči, ko so jih bili prižgali angeli in ki so plamtele pobožno *tam zunaj, globoko doli na zemlji.* (Cankar 1972:74)
>
> Leeming: They also saw out there the innumerable lights which the angels had lit for them and which blazed with a holy flame *down here on earth.* (Cankar 1976:98)

The hospital is no longer a part of this earth, it is *praeambula vitae aeternae* – it enables the girls to enter a new life. The fact that they do not feel connected with life on earth, especially at Christmas time, could not be seen in translation where the phrase "tam zunaj, globoko doli na zemlji" (LT: "outside, down there on earth"), emphasizing the distance between the lives of the girls and the life of the city, is translated with "down here on earth", which places everything, including the girls, in the earthly realm.

The vision of the third 'world' also gets blurred in the translation:

(11)   Tudi njena vera je bila trdna, vera v drug svet in v novo življenje in *tudi nji se je mudilo tja*, kjer sije resnično sonce in je vsa pokrajina neizmeren vrt ... (Cankar 1972:98)

Leeming: And her faith was firm, her faith in that other world, in that new life, so firm that *she felt no need to hurry* to that land where the real sun shone and all the countryside was one vast garden ... (Cankar 1976:131)

The sentence is taken from the passage describing the death of Malchie. The other girls have to postpone a long-awaited trip to the countryside and have to wait for her to die. In her dying vision, Malchie sees herself joining her friends in the ward on their trip which leads her to the Garden of Eden where Christ, her first and last lover, awaits her. Malchie wants to be united with her bridegroom and is therefore in a hurry – it is difficult to explain why Leeming translated the original "tudi nji se je mudilo tja" (LT: "she felt the need to hurry there") with the opposite "she felt no need to hurry" and made the original incomprehensible. Certainly, it would be difficult to argue that he mistook the affirmative for the negative form of the verb.

Other important translation shifts include extensions and omissions. Extensions do not usually change the understanding of the text, except in some cases:

(12)   Obšel jo je nemir, ker se ji je zazdelo, kakor da bi bili krenili vozovi na napačno pot – dol proti dolini, kjer je noč in trpljenje ... Ustnice so se gibale, vzkliknila je, ali glasu ni bilo. Tedaj se je ozrla Lojzka: "Glej, treba je skozi dolino ... *kako bi drugače gor*?" (Cankar 1972:99)

Leeming: She felt anxious because it seemed to her that the carriages had taken a dangerous turn – into a road which led downhill, to the place of night and suffering ... Her lips twisted and she tried to scream, but no sound came. Then Lois turned round and said, "Look, we've got to go downhill first ... *it's the only way to the hills!*" (Cankar 1976:133)

These sentences are also taken from the passage describing Malchie's dying visions, picturing herself and her friends on a trip to countryside. The passage could be understood as a description of a real trip the girls are going to make or as a metaphorical description of the voyage Malchie's soul is going to undertake at the time of death. Lois words "Glej, treba je skozi dolino ... *kako bi drugače gor*?" (LT: "Look, one has to go through the valley ... how else would one go up?") could also be understood as a reminder that Malchie has to die first before entering the eternal garden. Leeming's extension "it's the only way to the hills" limits the understanding of the passage to the description of a real voyage and makes the metaphorical understanding more difficult.

But the largest and most noticeable differences between the original and Leeming's translation are large omissions which remain unexplained and which the reader of the English translation is never cautioned about. The largest and most important for the understanding of the entire novel is the following:

(13)   Od vseh strani je zazvonilo, od vzhoda in od zahoda; od neizmernega neba so lile božične pesmi, vrele so iz zimske zemlje.

To je bil dan, ko se je rodil Človek in vsa srca so se odpirala njemu v hvalo in ljubezen, vse srca so zahrepenela k njemu.

Napotila so se k njemu tisočera užaljena, ranjena srca. Vsi ubogi, zaniče-vani, zavrženi so se napotili, brezkončna procesija je bila. Vsi tisti, ki jih je bilo življenje s trdo pestjo, so odprli trudne oči in so vzdignili ranjene ude, šli so in so mu nesli srca naproti. Križani Človek je sprejemal vse, na nikogar ni pozabil, ki se mu je približal, vsem je delil dragocene darove. In bili so mu hvaležni in so zaupali vanj. Dar, ki jim ga je bil podelil, je bil vreden več, nego vsa oskrunjena srca. Kogar se je dotaknila njegova usmiljena roka, kogar je blagoslovil njegov pogled, tisti je izpregledal, padlo mu je breme raz ramena, lahke in poskočne so bile njegove noge. Večni Človek mu je bil podelil večnost. Kadar so skeleli udarci življenja, je romalo srce k njemu, v deželo utolaženega upanja, pozabljenega trpljenja.

Zazvonili so božični zvonovi od vzhoda in od zahoda in vsepovsod so se dramili ranjeni in zavrženi in so vstajali. Trpljenje je praznovalo veliki praznik upanja in zmagoslavja; utolaženi so bili, ki so izpregledali, da vodi čez Kalvarijo cesta v veselo večnost. Ponosni so bili in so gledali zmagonosno, ko so vedeli, da so v njem in del njegov, zato ker so bičani in s trnjem kronani...

Tako so praznovali praznik, ko je nastopil Človek svojo veličastno pot. Ni ga bilo tisto noč ubogega srca, ki bi veselo ne vztrepetalo; komaj je razumelo radost, ki je kipela do vrha; komaj se je zavedal zaničevani in zavrženi in bilo mu je kakor v sanjah, ko je slišal tolažilne besede in ko je začutil usmiljeno roko na razgubanem čelu, na ramah, ranjenih od bremena.

Polna solz, krvi in gnusobe je sopla zemlja tam doli, v temi; ali glej, tisto noč je vzplamtelo tisočero in tisočero luči, vzdigali so se brezštevilni plameni, tresli so se in so plapolali in so hrepeneli gor...

"Nocoj hodijo angeli po zemlji," je dejala Tončka. (Cankar 1972: 73–74)

Leeming: The bells rang out on all sides, from east and west. The sounds of joyful Christmas songs surged up from the wintry earth and poured from the immensity of the sky.

"To-night the angels will walk among us," Toni said. (Cankar 1976: 98)

LT: The bells rang out on all sides, from east and west; the sounds of Christmas songs poured from the immensity of the sky, they surged up from the wintry earth.

This was the day when Man was born and all hearts opened for Him in praise and love, all hearts yearned for Him.

Thousands of offended, wounded hearts headed towards Him. All the miserable, the despised, the discarded headed towards Him, in an endless procession. All those who were battered by life opened their weary eyes and raised their wounded limbs, they went and brought Him their hearts. The crucified Man accepted everyone, He did not forget anyone who approached Him, He distributed precious gifts to everyone. And they were thankful and they trusted Him. The gift he gave was worthier than all the desecrated hearts. Whoever was touched by his merciful hand, whoever was blessed by his look saw, the burden fell off his shoulders, light and lively became his legs. The eternal man gave him eternity. When the strokes of life hurt, the heart went on a pilgrimage to Him, to the land of consoled hope, of forgotten suffering.

The Christmas bells rang out from east and west and on all sides the wounded and the discarded awakened and arose. Suffering celebrated the great holiday of hope and triumph; those who saw that a road into the merry eternity leads through Calvary were appeased. They were proud and had a triumphant look in their eyes because they knew that they are in Him and are His part, because they were flogged and crowned with thorns . . .

Thus they celebrated the holiday when Man set off on his magnificent path. There was not a miserable heart that evening that would not tremble in joy; it could hardly understand the happiness that surged up; the dispised and the discarded were hardly aware of it and they were like in a dream when they heard the words of solace and felt the merciful hand on the wrinkled brow, on their shoulders wounded by the heavy burden.

The earth full of tears, blood and abomination panted down there, in darkness; but look, that night thousands and thousands of lights lit up, numerous flames rose, they flickered and flared and yearned to go up . . .

"Tonight the angels walk on earth," Toni said.

Without any prior notice a large section is omitted at the beginning of Chapter 7 – the chapter that follows the disclosure of the sad histories of Tina, Lois, Brigid and Malchie, the stories about lonely childhood, adultery, paedophilia and crushed hopes. Cankar's insistence that his novel is not "filthy" but that when writing this work his thoughts were "as pure as spring water" (Izidor Cankar 1960:9–10), could be understood only in the light of the thought explained in those paragraphs, since only then the suffering of the sick girls becomes understandable. The omission of these important paragraphs profoundly influences our reading of the whole novel; without them it comes close to a purely naturalistic work depicting the sinister and squalid aspects of human nature, and almost completely loses its impressionistic, new romantic, religious character. The fourteen girls "waiting for life and health in death" (Iz. Cankar 1960:9–10), as the author described them, are the saviours of the fallen and corrupt world. All their suffering has not been in vain, because they are united with God. Moreover, with their suffering they help the Saviour and as a reward gain an insight into the joys of the life after death. Without this passage the novel becomes more naturalistic, which means that in the translation not only the message of the original was changed but also its tone.

The translation of the last sentence in the novel is also revealing:

(14)   Pozdravljen, Kristus, ženin, ti vdano ljubljeni, težko pričakovani! . . . Poz-
       dravljen! . . . (Cankar 1972:100)

       Leeming: Hail Jesus – dear Jesus. (Cankar 1976:133)

       LT: Hail, Christ, my bridegroom, my devotedly beloved, the long-awaited
       one! . . . Hail! . . .

With those last words Malchie dies and at the same time accepts Christ who is going to take her into the garden of eternal light. The words she uses are typical for Christian mystical tradition, in particular the metaphorical use of Christ as bridegroom eagerly expected by the soul which stems from the traditional interpretation of the Biblical *Song of Songs*. Malchie's death is not only the passage to a new life, but also the perfect mystical union with the Saviour. The fulfilment of the suffering lives of the children could then be found in the mystical union with Christ. Leeming in his translation tones down the conclusion and leaves out the emotional, erotic words – those changes, however, could not be explained by the claim that they are the result of cultural differences between Slovene and English culture, the description of the most perfect union with God through erotic imagery belongs to the common Christian tradition and could therefore also be found in English mystical literature. By avoiding the open description of Malchie's perfect union with God, the translation also tones down the mystical elements of the work and rewrites the novel in a more naturalistic vein.

When encountering culture-specific terms in the original (although they are extremely rare, most probably because the author wanted to stress the symbolic character of the hospital) the translator used different techniques. In the next example the original enumerates some of the mythical creatures from Slovene folk mythology:

(15)   /.../ mamca je bila, ki sedi za pečjo in pripoveduje bajke o vedomcu, o polnočnih strahovih, o beli ženi in torklji . . . (Cankar 1972:49)

Leeming: Here winter was an old nurse sitting by the stove, telling her ghost stories about witches, the spirits that walked at midnight, the lady in white, the spinning-wheel fairy . . . (Cankar 1976:65)

"Vedomec" is a person who leaves his body when asleep and becomes an evil spirit (SSKJ 5, 386); "bela žena" is a beautifal, female creature who lives in woods or in water, a kind of fairy (SSKJ 5, 988), "torklja" is a creature that punishes spinsters who spin in the evening on certain days (SSKJ 5, 127). Leeming exchanges the first culture-specific term with a culturally similar term in English (thus "vedomec" becomes "witches"), the second and the third are translated literally ("polnočni strahovi" becomes "the spirits that walked at midnight", "bela žena" is translated by "the lady in white"), for the last term an explanation is offered ("torklja" becomes "spinning-wheel fairy"), which skilfully keeps the meaning and clarity of the passage and at the same time retains the local flavour in the translation as well.

To conclude, it is difficult to give a simple answer to the question whether the shifts in Leeming's translation are those typical of non-native speakers of the source language and native speakers of the target language. Does the analysis reveal the translator's basic ignorance of the source language culture and language, as some might expect, or is this translation, because Henry Leeming is a competent native speaker of the target language and a person who knows the language of the original well, the best translation Slovene culture can hope for?

As far as the shifts concerning the punctuation, shortening of the sentences, and the distribution of sentences into paragraphs are concerned it would be difficult to argue that those changes are the result of the fact that the translator is a native speaker of the target language. Since Cankar's long sentences are not typical of the Slovene language as short sentences are not of the English language, it seems wise to acribe these stylistic changes consistently applied to entire translated text to the personal style of the translator.

Leeming's translation is also characterised by omissions. Some of them do not change the meaning of the text, others do. In particular, the largest omission of the five paragraphs at the beginning of Chapter 7 changes the novel profoundly and minimises its religious connotations, thus bringing the work more in line with the ideological stance of the state publishing house financing the translation. Similarly, the translation of the last sentence in the novel reveals that Leeming read and understood *The Ward of Our Lady of Mercy* as a naturalistic novel and therefore curtailed all the impressionistic and symbolic differentiation between the corrupt world of the city, the *praeambula vitae aeternae* in the hospital and the joyful world of life after death. Nor could this change be attributed to the fact that Leeming was a native speaker of English, since it is specific for this particular translator and should therefore not be generalized.

Extensions in Leeming's translation sometimes help the reader to understand culture-specific elements, sometimes they are the result of the translator's understanding and interpretation of the text: for example, in the passage where he interprets the voyage as a real trip to the countryside and avoids the ambiguity and the possibility of understanding the text as describing the final voyage Malchie's soul is going to undertake. In this case as well, it would be difficult to claim that such changes are typical for translators who are native speakers of English, since the shift is clearly the result of this specific translator's interpretation of the text.

When translating culturally-specific terms Leeming decides for a literal translation or for the use of a similar but general expression in English and does not resort to culturally-specific English expressions. He keeps many features of the original culture which, to be honest, are rarely present in the original. Here Leeming, as a native speaker of English and a member of a culture in which target-oriented translation is normative (see Venuti 1995), contrary to expectations, does not try to adapt the text as closely as possible to the target culture, but opts to retain Slovene culture-specific elements in the translation.

Through translation shifts that change the meaning of the novel, Leeming usually reveals his specific interpretation of it as a naturalistic work. Some changes cannot be explained and are perhaps the result of inaccurate reading of the original – such mistakes are characteristic not only of native speakers of the target language, they could be found in all the translations, regardless of the mother tongue of the translator. Only two instances were found where inaccurate translations might be the result of the fact that the translator was not a native speaker of the source language: i.e. when he did not recognise the archaic or the literary use of conjunctions.

If it is assumed that the translator who is a native speaker of the major target language and a non-native speaker of a minor source language should reveal his limited knowledge of the source language and culture and therefore try to adapt the text forcefully to the target culture – that is the general assumption on the potential flaws of translations by non-native speakers of the minor source language – then the analysis of Henry Leeming's *Ward of Our Lady of Mercy* shows, contrary to that position, that his translational shifts rarely give justification to such an assumption. On the other hand, the claim that a competent native speaker of the target language who knows well the source culture and language (like for example Henry Leeming) shall undoubtedly create an "impeccable" translation, again does not entirely correspond to the truth. Leeming's translation of *The Ward of Our Lady of Mercy* is specific, characterised by extensive omissions which are never acknowledged to the reader. Thus we may conclude that this translation does not answer the expectations of the first group of theoreticians who are suspicious of the non-native translators of the source language or the expectations of the second group who idolise the work of native speakers of the target language since every translation is largely, if not completely, the result of the individual convictions and strategies of a particular translator.

A Cup of Coffee by Louis Adamic

The translation of Cankar's *A Cup of Coffee* is one of Adamic's first translations into English. It was first published in July in 1922 in the journal *Overland Monthly*; in 1926 it was reprinted in *Mladinski list* (*Juvenile*), which was the publication of left-wing Slovene immigrants in the USA who were members of the organisation *Slovenska Narodna Podporna Jednota* (see Petrič 1978b: 39; Susel 1992: 239).

This translation of the sketch is the only one to have received some critical response: Jerneja Petrič (Petrič 1978a: 433–435, 1989: 52–53) claims that Adamic's "limited grasp of English" led to the translation failing to reflect Cankar's style and that the text was adapted and some passages shortened. She argues that at that time Adamic was "still developing his skills in English expression" (Petrič 1978a: 435, also 417), and that he started translating in order to enrich his vocabulary and develop his own style of writing in English (Petrič 1989: 51; see also Christian 1978: 223). And, indeed, in a letter to his publisher, Arthur Whipple, Adamic writes: "I am sending you a collection of short stories and shorter novels I translated between 1921 and 1923 when I was still 'wandering' around America and tried to write English the way I was able to." (Christian 1978:226) But despite some obvious linguistic difficulties the translator had, the analysis of the text reveals some deliberate changes of the text which are a result of a specific translational strategy and not so much his poor knowledge of the target language.

First let us look at some passages where Adamic's translation might be interpreted as the result of his poor knowledge of English or his careless reading of the original:

(1)   Tri ali štiri leta kasneje mi je v tujini tuja ženska prinesla kavo v sobo. (Cankar 1974:265)

Adamic: Three or four months later a strange woman brought me a cup of coffee to my room. (Cankar 1926a:83)

LT: Three of four years later a foreign woman brought coffee into my room.

Here Adamic translated "three or four years later" with "three or four month later", and since Adamic still knew Slovene at that time, his translation almost certainly reflected his careless reading of the original which resulted in this translational shift.

Adamic's translation is also characterised by omissions:

(2)   Nisem ji rekel ne zvečer, ne drugi dan in tudi ne ob slovesu … (Cankar 1974:265)

Adamic: But in the evening I could not speak to her kindly, nor the next day. (Cankar 1926a:83)

LT: I did not say anything to her that evening, nor the next day, nor when we parted …

In this case, the omission of "in tudi ne ob slovesu" ('nor when we parted') could be explained by the translator's limited knowledge of the target language, i.e. that he just did not know how to express this part of the sentence in English. Similarly, he avoids a problematic part in the following sentence:

(3)   Človek je v sami razmišljenosti hudoben in neusmiljen. (Cankar 1974:264)
      Adamic: Sometimes a person is merciless, cruel. (Cankar 1926a:82)

LT: When distracted, one can be malicious and merciless.

The next omission, however, could be explained by the translator's weak English or by the use of a specific translation strategy – Adamic left out parts of the text that are not linguistically difficult but the ones that could be considered as not essential to the development of the story. Adamic later described himself as a working-class writer writing for the working class, and argued in an article entitled "What the Proletariat Reads" that "not a few radical workers dislike the proletarian novels in which the authors' artistic mannerisms and tricks obscure what they wish to communicate" (Adamic 1934: 321–322). It is possible to interpret his modifications of the following passage where he left out everything in italics as deliberate changes to the meet the supposed taste of the proletariat:

(4) Preselil sem se pod streho, v seno. *V ta svoj dom sem plezal po strmih, polomljenih stopnicah, lestvi podobnih. Postlal sem si v senu, pred vrata na klanec sem si postavil mizo. Razgled moj je bil siv, razglodan zid.* V zli volji, v potrtosti in črnih skrbeh sem pisal takrat svoje prve zaljubljene zgodbe. (Cankar 1974: 263; emphasis by N. K. P.)

Adamic: I moved to the attic, where, in that dismal mood of mine, I began writing my first love stories. (Cankar 1926a: 82)

LT: I moved to the loft, among the hay. *Up to this home I used to climb by steep broken steps like those of a ladder. I made my bed in the hay, against the door which gave on to the slope I placed the table on. I looked out on to a grey crumbling wall.* In ill humour, depression and black thoughts I wrote my first love stories.

A specific translation strategy is also a more plausible reason for other quite extensive omissions at the beginning of the sketch:

(5) Velikokrat v svojem življenju sem storil krivico človeku, ki sem ga ljubil. <u>Taka krivica je kakor greh zoper svetega duha: ne na tem, ne na onem svetu ni odpuščena.</u> Neizbrisljiva je, nepozabljiva. Včasi počiva dolga leta, kakor da je bila ugasnila v srcu, izgubila se, utopila v nemirnem življenju. Nenadoma, sredi vesele ure, ali ponoči, ko se prestrašen vzdramiš iz hudih sanj, pade v dušo težak spomin, zaboli in zapeče s toliko silo, kakor da je bil greh šele v tistem trenotku storjen. Vsak drug spomin je lahko zabrisati s kesanjem in z blago mislijo – tega ni mogoče zabrisati. Črn madež je na srcu in ostane na vekomaj.

Rad bi človek lagal sem sebi v dušo: "Saj ni bilo tako! Le tvoja nemirna misel je iz prosojne sence napravila noč! Malenkost je bila, vsakdanjost, kakor se jih sto in tisoč vrši od jutra do večera!"

Tolažba je zlagana; in človek občuti sam in z grenkobo, da je zlagana. Greh je greh, če je storjen enkrat ali tisočkrat, če je vsakdanji ali nepoznan. Srce ni kazenski zakonik, da bi razločevalo med pregreškom in hudodelstvom, med ubojem in umorom. Srce ve, da "zavratnež ubija s pogledom, z mečem junak"; in rajše bi dalo odvezo meču nego pogledu. Tudi ni srce katekizem, da bi razločevalo med njimi po besedi in zunanjih znamenjih. Srce je pravičen in nezmotljiv sodnik. *Sodi in obsodi grešnika po skriti, komaj zavedni kretnji, po hipnem pogledu, ki ga nihče ni opazil, po neizgovorjeni, komaj na čelu zapisani misli; celo po koraku, po trkanju na duri, po srebanju čaja. Le malo grehov je napisanih v katekizmu in še tisti niso poglavitni. Če bi bilo srce izpovednik – dolga in strašna bi bila izpoved!*

Odpustljiv je greh, ki ga je mogoče povedati z besedo, izbrisati ga s pokoro. Težak in pretežak, do zadnje ure krvaveč je greh, ki je ostal samo v srcu kakor spomin brez besede in brez oblike. Le sam sebi ga človek izpoveduje, kadar strmi v noč in mu je odeja na prsih težja od kamena.

"Ne kradel nisem, ne ubijal, ne prešestoval; čista je moja duša!"

Lažnivec! Ali nisi lupil jabolka, ko si šel mimo lačnega ter si pogledal brez sramu? Hujše je bilo, nego da si kradel, ubijal in prešestoval! Pravični sodnik, srce, bo rajše odpustilo ubijavcu, ki je gredoč na vislice pobožal jokajočega otroka, nego tebi čistemu! Zakaj srce ne pozna malenkosti in tudi ne paragrafov . . . (Cankar 1974: 262–263; all emphases in quotations are mine)

Adamič: I have often been unjust, unfair to people whom I loved. <u>Such injustice is an unpardonable sin, permanent, enduring, unforgettable in one's conscience</u>. Sometimes the sin is as forgotten, eroded from your life, drowned in the eventfulness of the days; but suddenly, perhaps in the middle of a beautiful enjoyable day, perhaps at night, it comes back upon you, to weigh down your soul, to pain and burn your conscience as though you have just committed it. Almost every other sin or bitter memory may be washed away with atonement and good thought, except this sin of injustice against someone whom you love. It becomes a black mar on your heart and there it remains.

A man may perhaps try to lie to his soul. "It wasn't so bad as that. Your restlessness has created a black night out of mere shadows. It was but a trifle, an every-day occurrence." . . . Such words are lies, and the man knows it. The heart is not a penal code in which crimes and offenses are defined. Nor is it a catechism, in which sins are classified. The human heart is a judge just and consistent.

Pardonable is a sin which can be described by a word of mouth and atoned for. But heavy, tremendously heavy, is a sin which remains with you – in your heart – indescribable, formless. You confess it to yourself when you tremble in fear before death, or at night when the covers of your bed seem like mountain piles upon you. (Cankar 1926a: 82)

LT: Often in my life I have done harm to a person I loved. <u>This is like a sin against the Holy Ghost; neither in this nor in the other world can it be forgiven</u>. It can never be blotted out, never forgotten. Sometimes it lies unfelt for long years as if it had burned itself out in the heart, as if it were lost, submerged in the restlessness of life. All at once, in the midst of some happy hour or at night, when one wakes with a start from a bad dream, there falls on the soul the burden of a memory, burning as painfully and as deeply as if the sin had been committed that very moment. All other memories may be erased with repentance and with gentle thoughts – this alone cannot be erased. It is a dark stain on the heart and remains so for ever more.

One would like to be able to lie to one's soul, to say "It was not like that. It is only your restless mind making dark nights out of the lightest of shadows. It was such a little thing, the sort of thing that happens every day, a hundred or a thousand times between morning and evening!"

But the consolation is false; and man feels, personally and with bitterness, that it is false. Sin is sin, be it committed once or a thousand times, be it a thing of every day or one unknown. The heart is not the penal code with its distinctions between crime and misdemeanour, between murder and manslaughter. The heart knows that "a traitor kills with a look, a hero with a sword", and will rather pardon the sword than the look. Nor is the heart the catechism with its distinctions between venial and capital sins, with its distinctions by words and by outward signs. The heart is a righteous and infallible judge. *It judges and sentences the sinner by a secret, scarcely observable movement, by a momentary glance of which no-one has been aware, by an unuttered thought scarcely traceable upon the brow; even by a step, by a knock on the door, by a sip of tea. Only a few sins are defined in the catechism and those not the chiefest. If the heart were a confessor – long and dreadful would that confession be!*

Pardonable is the sin which may be told in words, redeemed by penance. A wound, a dire wound, bleeding till the final hour is the sin which has remained in the heart as a memory, wordless and formless. Only to himself does man confess, gazing into the night, the blanket upon his breast heavier than stone.

"I have never stolen, nor killed, nor committed adultery; my soul is pure!"

Liar! Did you not peel an apple as you passed a hungry man and look at him without shame? That was worse than if you had stolen, killed or committed adultery! That righteous judge, the heart, will rather forgive the murderer who in the shadow of the gallows comforted a weeping child than you, the pure one. For the heart knows no trifles and also no provisions of the law. (adapted from the translation by E. Jereb & A. MacKinnon in Cankar 1971a: 140–141)

The sentences in italics are not translated in Adamic's version. It seems hardly possible that Adamic avoided the translation of those passages because he did not know how to express them in English, especially because also later on when his English was much stronger (in fact so strong that he claimed that he had lost his Slovene and replaced it with English) omissions and extensions were an essential part of his translation strategy (see Kocijančič 1993, 1999). Most probably in this case as well, he considered those passages as the author's "artistic mannerisms and tricks" which obscure what he wishes to communicate (Adamic 1934: 321–322). Adamic later on directed his interventions in particular towards changing or omitting passages that were too explicitly religious. And this early translation already anticipates such changes – the underlined sentence is thus translated using more neutral expressions in English: "This is like a sin against the Holy Ghost; neither in this nor in the other world can it be forgiven" becomes "Such injustice is an unpardonable sin, permanent, enduring, unforgetable in one's conscience", where "the Holy Ghost", "this and the other world" are not mentioned, and "conscience" is introduced. With this shift the translator emphasizes that we shall ultimately answer to our conscience and not to God, and thus according to his personal views transfers the reader from the realm of divine justice to the human one.

He also adds some elements to the text:

(6)   Pust in zlovoljen, brez besede in pozdrava sem se vrnil pod streho, da bi pisal, kako sta se ljubila Milan in Breda in kako sta bila obadva plemenita, srečna in vesela.
      "Roko v roki, obadva mlada, od jutranjega sonce obžarjena, v rosi umita . . ." (Cankar 1974: 264)

Adamic: After I informed her that I wanted some black coffee, I returned to the attic to continue my love story, to write how Milan and Breda loved each other, how noble, divine, happy and joyful they were... "Hand in hand, both young and athrob with life, bathed in morning dew-drops, swaying –" (Cankar 1926a: 82)

LT: Sour and ill-humoured, without as much as a word I went up to my loft to write about the love of Milan and Breda, and how noble, fortunate, happy and merry they both were.
      "Hand in hand, both young, illuminated by the morning sun, bathed in dew . . .".

Besides joining two paragraphs into one, Adamic also adds that Milan and Breda were "divine", introduces a neologism "athrob with life" meaning 'throbbing with life', and extends the text at the end with "swaying" – which all reveals a considerable self-confidence of the translator in the target language, so much so that he dares introduce new words into the language.

Although less daring, his extensions of the text are present everywhere, including in the last sentence of the sketch:

(7)   Zakaj srce je pravičen sodnik in ne pozna malenkosti . . . (Cankar 1974: 265)

    Adamic: For a man's heart is a just and consistent judge; a man's heart does not concern itself with paragraphs and provisions in statute books or trifles. (Cankar 1926a: 83)

    LT: For the heart is a righteous judge and knows no trifles . . .

Instead of Biblical terseness and the conclusion that something that seems a mere trifle for someone can be the most painful sin for the other, Adamic offers the translation of the final sentence overburdened with legal expressions he should have but did not include in the passage quoted above in example (6).

Louis Adamic as a representative of non-native translators in many ways supports the claims of those translation theoreticians who argue that all inverse translations are defective and that they sound foreign and unacceptable to native speakers of the TL. But even more than linguistic awkwardness, Adamic's translation manifests a specific approach to translation, according to which the text can and should be freely reformulated according to the translator's poetological and ideological views. Moreover, it seems that the most crucial translation shifts which effect the understanding of the sketch are due to his specific translation strategy and not so much to his negligence or poor knowledge of English.

A Cup of Coffee by Agata Zmajić and M. Peters-Roberts

The sketch *A Cup of Coffee* was also translated by a Croatian, Agata Zmajić, and M. Peters-Roberts, who was most probably a native speaker of English. The translation was first published in the London *Review of Reviews* in 1933. Although almost nothing is known about the creation of the sketch, the translation is interesting because it was translated by two non-native speakers of the SL. Their translation strategy can already be detected in the introductory sentences:

(1)   Velikokrat v svojem življenju sem storil krivico človeku, ki sem ga ljubil. Taka krivica je kakor greh zoper svetega duha: ne na tem, ne na onem svetu ni odpuščena. Neizbrisljiva je, nepozabljiva. Včasi počiva dolga leta, kakor da je bila ugasnila v srcu, izgubila se, utopila v nemirnem življenju. Nenadoma, sredi vesele ure, ali ponoči, ko se prestrašen vzdramiš iz hudih sanj, pade v dušo težak spomin, zaboli in zapeče s toliko silo, kakor da je bil greh šele v tistem trenotku storjen. Vsak drug spomin je lahko zabrisati s kesanjem in z blago mislijo – tega ni mogoče zabrisati. Črn madež je na srcu in ostane na vekomaj.

Rad bi človek lagal sem sebi v dušo: "Saj ni bilo tako! *Le tvoja nemirna misel je iz prosojne sence napravila noč!* Malenkost je bila, vsakdanjost, kakor se jih sto in tisoč vrši od jutra do večera!"

Tolažba je zlagana; in človek občuti sam in z grenkobo, da je zlagana. Greh je greh, če je storjen enkrat ali tisočkrat, če je vsakdanji ali nepoznan. Srce ni kazenski zakonik, da bi razločevalo med pregreškom in hudodelstvom, med ubojem in umorom. Srce ve, da "zavratnež ubija s pogledom, z mečem junak"; in rajše bi dalo odvezo meču nego pogledu. Tudi ni srce katekizem, da bi razločevalo med njimi po besedi in zunanjih znamenjih. Srce je pravičen in nezmotljiv sodnik. Sodi in obsodi grešnika po skriti, komaj zavedni kretnji, po hipnem pogledu, ki ga nihče ni opazil, po neizgovorjeni, komaj na čelu zapisani misli; celo po koraku, po trkanju na duri, po srebanju čaja. Le malo grehov je napisanih v katekizmu in še tisti niso poglavitni. Če bi bilo srce izpovednik – dolga in strašna bi bila izpoved!

Odpustljiv je greh, ki ga je mogoče povedati z besedo, izbrisati ga s pokoro. Težak in pretežak, do zadnje ure krvaveč je greh, ki je ostal samo v srcu kakor spomin brez besede in brez oblike. Le sam sebi ga človek izpoveduje, kadar strmi v noč in *mu je odeja na prsih težja od kamena.*

"Ne kradel nisem, ne ubijal, ne prešestoval; čista je moja duša!"

Lažnivec! Ali nisi lupil jabolka, ko si šel mimo lačnega ter si pogledal brez sramu? Hujše je bilo, nego da si kradel, ubijal in prešestoval! Pravični sodnik, srce, bo rajše odpustilo ubijavcu, ki je gredoč na vislice pobožal jokajočega otroka, nego tebi čistemu! *Zakaj srce ne pozna malenkosti in tudi ne paragrafov* ... (Cankar 1974: 262–263)

Zmajić & Peters-Roberts: Dᴜʀɪɴɢ my life I have often grieved someone I dearly loved. It is my belief that this is like the sin against the Holy Ghost, which "shall not be forgiven him, neither in this world, neither in the world to come".

The memory of it may remain asleep for many years, almost forgotten in the whirl and turmoil of everyday life. Then, all of a sudden – it may be in the midst of a scene of gaiety, or, in the dead of night during a terrible dream – it awakes, to weigh heavily on the soul, to burn and torment as if it had only been committed a moment before.

Other memories can be blotted out by good deeds, holy thoughts, and deep repentance, but this – never. It remains always a dark blot on the soul. How gladly would man salve his conscience, would try to belittle the offence .... "It was not quite as bad as all that ... *It is your over-sensitiveness that had magnified a small fault into a sin ....* Why, it was merely a trifle, which happens many times a day between sunrise and sunset ...." But this is only false comfort, for he knows perfectly well, and also feels bitterly, that he is only deluding himself. The offence remains the same, whether committed seldom or often, once or a thousand times.

THE heart is not a penal Book of Law, distinguishing between offences and crimes, between killing and murder. It acknowledges that the hero destroys with the sword, but so does the traitor with a look, and the first is pardoned rather than the last.

Neither is the heart like the Church Catechism, which separates sins into small and great, into mortal and venial. The heart is a righteous, incorruptible Judge which sentences and condemns the secret impulse, barely recognized; the swift glance which nobody sees, the fleeting unexpressed thought; and it even judges the way of walking, knocking at the door, or drinking tea. *It is a searching Judge, who probes into the innermost recesses of our being.*

NOT all sins, and certainly not the weightiest, are contained in the Catechism. Were our heart to act as Confessor, what a long and terrible confession it would have to hear.

Sins which can be confessed in words, and cleansed by repentance, may find forgiveness, but those never admitted, never mentioned, will remain like nebulous, unformed shapes to burden our souls to the end of our life. These are the sins which man only admits to himself when he lies awake at night, staring into the darkness, and feeling *as if the ceiling were about to crush down upon him.*

"I have never stolen nor killed, neither have I committed adultery .... My soul is clean!"

Liar! Did you not look with indifference on the face of a hungry man when you passed him, peeling you apple? This is worse than stealing, killing or committing adultery. A murderer who stops to caress a weeping child on his way to execution will be forgiven sooner than you, you clean soul! (Cankar 1933b: 52)

At first glance the translation shows a new organisation of the text: the paragraph divisions do not correspond to those of the original. The translators also change the original punctuation; particularly interesting is the fact that they put in inverted commas those parts of the text they felt to be closely following Biblical wording (see e.g. the first paragraph). Some of the changes also modify the tone of the text towards a more objective mood and moderate the poetical features of the original, for example: "Le tvoja nemirna misel je iz prosojne sence napravila noč!" (LT: It is only your restless thought making dark night out of the lightest of shadows!) becomes "It is your over-sensitiveness that had magnified a small fault into a sin ....", which conveys the same meaning but in more prosaic terms. Similarly, the next underlined example: "Le sam sebi ga človek izpoveduje, kadar strmi v noč in *mu je odeja na prsih težja od kamena*," (LT: Only to himself does man confess, gazing into the night, *the blanket upon his breast heavier than stone*.) becomes "These are the sins which man only admits to himself when he lies awake at night, staring into the darkness, and feeling *as if the ceiling were about to crush down upon him*."

The translators also omit the last sentence ("Zakaj srce ne pozna malenkosti in tudi ne paragrafov ...", LT: For the heart knows no trifles and also no provisions of the law.) and add a sentence: "It is a searching Judge, who probes into the innermost recesses of our being." Those changes, however, do not affect the understanding nor the meaning of the sketch – they seem to be the result of a specific translation strategy and could not be classified as shifts typical of non-native speakers of the source language.

However, some of the changes could be expained by the fact that neither translator was a native speaker of Slovene:

(2)   Postlal sem si v senu, pred vrata na klanec sem si postavil mizo. Razgled moj je bil siv, razglodan zid. (Cankar 1974: 263)

Zmajić & Peters-Roberts: Here I arranged a bed in the hay, and placed a table near the door, so that I could have a view of the mountains while I worked. On my other side was a grey, crumbling wall. (Cankar 1933b: 53)

LT: I made my bed in the hay, against the door which gave on to the slope I placed the table. I looked out on to a grey crumbling wall.

The translation by Zmajić and Peters-Roberts adds that the narrator had a view of the mountains while he worked and thus introduces a (largely stereotypical) Alpine element into the story. The original stresses the fact that the young writer could only look at the grey, crumbling wall, which is still included in the translated text but it no longer represents the complete opposite to the imaginary world of the writer of the love story, since it no longer limits the narrator's view. This shift could be explained by the translators failing to understand the phrase "pred vrata na klanec" (LT: "against the door which gave on to the slope") and therefore changing the text in translation.

The next example is also interesting:

(3)   Človek je v sami razmišljenosti hudoben in neusmiljen. (Cankar 1974: 264)

Zmajić & Peters-Roberts: Lack of imagination can make a man cruel and wicked. (Cankar 1933b: 53)

LT: When distracted, one can be malicious and merciless.

Their translation of the word "razmišljenost" (which is defined by the *Slovene Dictionary* as 'raztresenost', i.e. 'distraction', 'heedlessness', 'inadvertence' (SSKJ 4, 378)) by "lack of imagination" might be explained by the fact that they were not native speakers of Slovene and did not know the word in question. However, those two cases were the only instances where it could be argued that the fact that the translators were non-native speakers of Slovene influenced their translation.

All in all, *A Cup of Coffee* by Agata Zmajić and M. Peters-Roberts could be defined as a meticulous, thorough translation. It is characterised by a reorganisation of the paragraphs of the text, and by a partial toning down of some of its poetical features. The translation does not completely correspond to the assumption that translators who are not native speakers of the source language fail to understand the original and therefore often change the meaning of the text – those "mistakes" are very rare and they only occur in places which are not essential for the understanding of the sketch and do not change the style or the tone of the original.

A Cup of Coffee by Jože Paternost

Jože Paternost translated *A Cup of Coffee* for the right-wing newspaper of Slovene immigrants in the USA, *Ameriška domovina,* in 1957, i.e. 12 years after he and his family left Slovenia for good. The translation was published on page 6, squeezed among various advertisements and jokes. The translation seems sloppy; it is often inaccurate, and many of the more difficult passages are simply omitted:

(1) Postlal sem si v senu, pred vrata na klanec sem si postavil mizo. Razgled moj je bil siv, razglodan zid. (Cankar 1974:263)

Paternost: I made a bed in the hay and placed my table before the door. My only view was a grey, corroded wall. (Cankar 1957a:6)

"Pred vrata na klanec" (LT: "against the door which gave on to the slope") – a phrase which proved problematic to other translators – is simply omitted. Similarly, Paternost does not translate the adjective "plemenita":

(2) Pust in zlovoljen, brez besede in pozdrava sem se vrnil pod streho, da bi pisal, kako sta se ljubila Milan in Breda in kako sta bila obadva *plemenita*, srečna in vesela. (Cankar 1974:264)

Paternost: Ill-humored and peevish, without a word I returned under the roof in order to write how Milan and Breda loved each other and how they were so happy and gay. (Cankar 1957a:6)

LT: Sour and ill-humoured, without as much as a word I went up to my loft to write about the love of Milan and Breda, and how noble, fortunate, happy and merry they both were.

The adjective "plemenita" (i.e. 'noble') proved difficult for some translators since it is not clear whether it refers to the social status or the state of mind of the two main characters in the narrator's novel (although nobility of mind is more plausible in view of Cankar's other works). Paternost's translation also reveals awkwardness in English expression – his literal translation "I returned under the roof" of the Slovene phrase "iti pod streho" meaning 'going up to the loft' is questionable and hardly understandable in English. But it gets even worse; in the next example his translation conveys just the opposite of the original message:

(3) Človek je v sami razmišljenosti hudoben in neusmiljen. (Cankar 1974:264)

Paternost: A man is in his very thoughtfulness malicious and cruel. (Cankar 1957a:6)

LT: When distracted, one can be malicious and merciless.

Most probably Paternost wanted to write "thoughtlessness" and not "thoughtfulness", since it makes little sense that thoughtfulness can make us malicious and cruel to others.

The next change of meaning is also interesting:

(4) Ustnice so se smehljale kakor otroku, ki prinaša vesel dar. (Cankar 1974: 264)

Paternost: She smiled as if to a child to whom she was bringing a joyful gift. (Cankar 1957a: 6)

LT: Her lips smiled like those of a child bringing a happy gift.

It seems as if the translator did not understand the original text, although he is a native speaker of Slovene. Cankar compared the mother to a child carrying a happy gift – Paternost translated the passage so that in his version the mother smiles like a mother bringing the child a joyful gift, which makes the comparison pointless, since she is a mother bringing her child a gift.

To conclude, besides a limited mastery of English, Paternost's translation also reveals negligent reading of the original or even a possible misunderstanding of the Slovene text (in fact, his misunderstandings are much more crucial than those detected in the work by two non-native speakers of Slovene, Agata Zmajić in M. Peters-Roberts) which completely undermines theoretical assumptions of the innate capacities every native speaker should have had.

A Cup of Coffee by Elza Jereb and Alasdair MacKinnon

The last translation of this sketch included in the questionnaire is the work of a pair of translators, consisting of a native speaker of the source language, Elza Jereb, and a native speaker of the target language, Alasdair MacKinnon. The translation was published in 1971 in Ljubljana by the state publishing house Državna založba Slovenije in a volume entitled Ivan Cankar *My Life and Other Sketches*. The selection of the sketches and the introduction were the work of Josip Vidmar, the most prominent literary critic of the post-Second-World-War period in Slovenia. The book includes, in addition to the sketch mentioned in the title, a selection of sketches from the last period of Cankar's life, in particular from his *Dream Visions*. The front page announces that the sketches were selected by Josip Vidmar, who is the President of the Slovene Academy of Science thus providing the "academic" guarantee that this selection is in fact representative of Cankar's work.

In his introduction, Josip Vidmar claims that Cankar represents not only the peak of the literary current called the Slovene *Moderna* but also of Slovene prose in general. He compares his work with that of Ibsen, Nietzsche, Oscar Wilde, Verlaine and Baudelaire and claims that Cankar's work reveals "no Russian influence" – although Cankar in his correspondence often confessed that he was a great admirer of Dostoyevsky and Tolstoy, which Vidmar almost certainly knew. It seems as if Vidmar wanted to stress Slovene independence from Russian influence as such and present Cankar as a part of the Western and not Eastern literary tradition. He stresses Cankar's belief in the purity of humanity exemplified in the notion of the mother; the devotion and indignation he felt towards his nation (Vidmar also briefly presents the historical and political reality Cankar lived through); and finally his protest against social injustice typical of the early capitalism spreading throughout Slovene lands during his lifetime. He also gives a short biography of Cankar and stresses that he found his only solace in Socialism and "an essentially non-materialistic religion of longing" (Vidmar 1971: 11). The introduction stresses that Cankar's work was too revolutionary in form and spirit for his time and that the contemporary critics therefore often rejected his work; but that the posterity recognised his greatness (Vidmar even mentions Partisan brigades carrying his name during the Second World War) and that future generations found in him their predecessor. Vidmar concludes his introduction by saying that the aim of this selection was to represent as comprehensively as possible the variety of Cankar's sketches (Vidmar 1971: 7–13).

The sketches in this selection are all openly source-oriented. Thus the translation of *A Cup of Coffee* reveals the typical features of Jereb and MacKinnon's translation strategy. For example, the original paragraph divisions of the text are retained in the translation. No misunderstandings of the original or changes of meaning, and no extensive omissions or additions were recorded. All the passages that proved problematic to other translators did not seem to have caused any problems to them:

(1)   Postlal sem si v senu, pred vrata na klanec sem si postavil mizo. Razgled moj je bil siv, razglodan zid. (Cankar 1974: 263)

Jereb and MacKinnon: I made my bed in the hay. Against the door which gave on to the slope I stood the table. I looked out on to a grey crumbling wall. (Cankar 1971a: 142)

In contrast to other translators mentioned above, Jereb and MacKinnon do not avoid translating the phrase "pred vrata na klanec". Nor does the translation of the word "razmišljenost" seem problematic to them:

(2)   Človek je v sami razmišljenosti hudoben in neusmiljen. (Cankar 1974: 264)

Jereb and MacKinnon: Out of pure inadvertence man may be evil and pitiless. (Cankar 1971a: 142)

They have also recognised the ambiguity of the word "plemenit" ('noble') and kept it in their translation:

(3)   Pust in zlovoljen, brez besede in pozdrava sem se vrnil pod streho, da bi pisal, kako sta se ljubila Milan in Breda in kako sta bila obadva plemenita, srečna in vesela. (Cankar 1974: 264)

Jereb and MacKinnon: Sour and full of ill humour, without as much as a word I went up to my loft to write about the love of Milan and Breda, and how noble, fortunate, happy and gay they both were. (Cankar 1971a: 142)

The translation by Elza Jereb and Alasdair MacKinnon does not fit into any of the presupposed categories; it is faithful to the original but at the same time fluent in the target language; it does not reveal any problems the translators might have had in understanding the original text, and at the same time it avoids excessive foreignness in the target language. Unfortunately, in the passage used in the questionnaire, there occurs a printing mistake (instead of "I recall now that she was never as beautiful as at that moment" the text has "I recall now hat (sic!) she was never as beautiful as at that moment") which influenced many of the subjects interviewed.

Children and Old People by Anthony J. Klančar

Anthony J. Klančar published his translation of the sketch *Children and Old People* (*Otroci in starci*) in 1933 in the English section of the left-wing journal of Slovene immigrants in the USA *Nova doba – New Era*. The translation shares the page with Labor Day greetings addressed to the readers by the Secretary of Labor, Frances Perkins.

In the editor's note, we learn that the sketch *Children and Old Age* (sic!) was taken from Cankar's *Dream Visions*, the last and most important work by the great Slovene novelist. It is added that the sketches were published in 1917 and that they reflect the author's impressions of the First World War. The editor then also mentions that the work has been translated into Russian, Czech and Italian, and that some of the sketches have recently been translated into French. In the last sentence we learn that in Slovene literary history Cankar's works are seen as either naturalistic or Decadent and Symbolic (Cankar 1933a: 7).

Klančar's translation closely follows the original; it retains almost completely the original paragraph divisions and punctuation (in only one case does he join two paragraphs). His translation is source-oriented and almost *verbatim* follows the original wording:

> (1)   Otroci so imeli navado, da so se pogovarjali, preden so šli spat. Posedli so po široki peči in so si pripovedovali, kar jim je pač prišlo na misel. Skozi motna okna je gledal v izbo večerni mrak z očmi, polnimi sanj, iz vseh kotov so se vile kvišku tihe sence in so nosile prečudne bajke s seboj. (Cankar 1975: 21)
>
> Klančar: The children were in the habit of conversing before they went to sleep. They sat for awhile on a broad, flat stove and told each other what happened to occur to them. Evening dusk peeped into the room through dim windows, with its eyes full of dreams; the silent shadows writhed upward from all corners and carried off their extremely wonderful fairy tales. (Cankar 1933a: 6)

However, Klančar tended to use words of different register and style in all of his translations: very formal and rarely-used words are often found in a colloquial surrounding (e.g. in the above-quoted example the use of "conversing" for an unmarked word in Slovene "pogovarjali" (LT: 'talked')). This passage also reveals that because Klančar was a member of the second generation of Slovene immigrants in the USA, he already had troubles understanding the Slovene original. For example, in the original we read that "iz vseh kotov so se vile kvišku tihe sence in so nosile prečudne bajke s seboj" (LT: "out of every corner the silent shadows drifted upwards, carrying strange fairy tales with them"), where the translator must have understood "prečudne" (LT: "strange", "very strange") as "prečudovite" (LT: "wonderful", "extremely wonderful") and translated it wrongly.

With regard to Slovene names, the translator decided to retain them:

> (2)   Otroci so si bili tako podobni med seboj, da se v mraku ni prav nič razločil obraz najmlajšega, štiriletnega Tončka, od obraza desetletne Lojzke, najstarejše med njimi. (Cankar 1975: 21)
>
> Klančar: The children resembled each other so much that in the twilight one could not at all distinguish the visage of Tonchek, the youngest, a boy of 4, from the visage of Lojzka, the eldest, a girl of 10. (Cankar 1933a: 6)

He translated "Tonček" and "Lojzka" with "Tonchek" and "Lojzka", changing only the spelling of the first name in order to assure the right pronunciation. However, he is not consistent in his foreignization:

> (3)   Matijče je razložil /.../. (Cankar 1975: 22)
>
> Klančar: Matija explained /.../. (Cankar 1933a: 6)

In this case he changed the dialectal variant "Matijče" with its unmarked literary version "Matija" – he most probably found the form of the proper name in the original too foreign for the target audience.

Some solutions also reveal that he had problems with English as well:

(4) Pošta je bila oznanila, da je oče "padel" na Laškem. "Padel je." (Cankar 1975:21)

Klančar: The post had sent notice that father "fell" in Italy. "He fell." (Cankar 1933a:6)

(5) Stara dva sta sedela globoko sključena, tesno drug ob drugem in sta se držala za roko, kakor že dolgo ne poprej; gledala sta nebeško zarjo večerno z očmi brez solz in nista rekla nobene besede. – (Cankar 1975:24)

Klančar: The two old people sat bent low, tightly side by side, and held each other's hands as they had once a long time before; they gazed at the dying sunset with tearless eyes and said nothing. (Cankar 1933a:6)

In example (5) the sequence of tenses could be applied so that the Past Tense should be changed into the Past Perfect Tense, in example (5) the elliptical sentence "as they had once" seems too elliptical and would require the use of the substitute verb "do" or the repetition of the verb.

To sum up, Klančar's translation of the sketch *Children and Old People* closely follows the original text: it almost completely reproduces the original paragraph divisions and punctuation. The translator has some difficulties with English, e.g. he sometimes combines words of different register and has some grammatical problems; it is also possible that he had problems understanding the Slovene text. When translating culture-specific terms, the translator opts for the foreignisation of the text and retains those terms in his translation, which could be explained by the fact that the text was published in a bilingual journal for Slovenian immigrants to the USA. This explanation, however, should be treated with caution. The target audience does not always prove to be a defining factor for the choice of the general strategy or method assumed by the translator, particularly in Klančar's case. Thus, for example, Klančar employed several opposing strategies in the same year in the same journal: e.g. in his translation of another short story by Ivan Cankar entitled *Sonce! ... Sonce! (The Sun! ... The Sun!* (Cankar 1933:6)), published in the above-mentioned Slovene immigrant journal *New Era,* he used a mixture of foreignising and domesticating strategies, and later in the same year a domesticating strategy in his translation of Cankar's *Rue de nations* (Cankar

1933:6). It can be argued, then, that the choice of translation strategy is not necessarily influenced by the target audience for the translation.

Children and Old People by A. J. Klančar and George R. Noyes

Anthony J. Klančar revised the translation discussed above with an American linguist G. R. Noyes in 1933/34 and published it with four other sketches (i.e. *The Captain, The Sun … The Sun …, The Dead will not Allow It*, and *Rue de nations*) under the title *Slovene Idylls* in the journal *The Slavonic Review*.

The revised *Children and Old People* smooths out all the stylistic lapses of the previous version:

(1)   Otroci so imeli navado, da so se pogovarjali, preden so šli spat. Posedli so po široki peči in so si pripovedovali, kar jim je pač prišlo na misel. Skozi motna okna je gledal v izbo večerni mrak z očmi, polnimi sanj, iz vseh kotov so se vile kvišku tihe sence in so nosile prečudne bajke s seboj. (Cankar 1975:21)

Klančar and Noyes: The children were in the habit of talking together before they went to sleep. They sat for awhile on a broad, flat stove and told one another whatever happened to occur to them. The evening dusk peered into the room through dim windows, with its eyes full of dreams; the silent shadows writhed upward from every corner and carried away with them their marvellous fairy tales. (Cankar 1933/34a:494)

While Klančar and Noyes in their revised translation replace the awkward word "conversing" with a more neutral expression "talking", they still keep "marvellous fairy tales" (they do however drop "extremely") which gives evidence that the translation was only stylistically revised and was not retranslated as such – Noyes only modified the style and did not check the original as far as the meaning was concerned.

Noyes's stylistic improvements, however, did not orient the text completely towards the target culture: e.g. this adapted translation still keeps the culture-specific proper names:

(2)   Otroci so si bili tako podobni med seboj, da se v mraku ni prav nič razločil obraz najmlajšega, štiriletnega Tončka, od obraza desetletne Lojzke, najstarejše med njimi. (Cankar 1975:21)

Klančar and Noyes: The children so much resembled one another that in the twilight one could not distinguish the countenance of Tonček, the youngest, a boy of four, from that of Lojzka, the oldest, a girl of ten. (Cankar 1933/34a:494)

Moreover, this translation does not change the spelling of the names like Klančar did in his first version and keeps the original Slovene diacritical mark. Another proof that Noyes most probably did not check the original is the next example:

(3)   Matijče je razložil /.../. (Cankar 1975: 22)

Klančar and Noyes: Matija explained /.../. (Cankar 1933/34a: 495)

Although the revised translation tried to keep the original spelling of the proper names, in this case not only the spelling but the name itself is changed from the dialectal version "Matijče" into "Matija" following Klančar's decision in his first translation.

But despite the fact that the text was not retranslated, it was nevertheless stylistically and grammatically revised:

(4)   Pošta je bila oznanila, da je oče "padel" na Laškem. "Padel je." (Cankar 1975: 21)

Klančar and Noyes: The post had brought notice that father "had fallen" in Italy. "He had fallen." (Cankar 1933/34a: 494)

(5)   Stara dva sta sedela globoko sključena, tesno drug ob drugem in sta se držala za roko, kakor že dolgo ne poprej; gledala sta nebeško zarjo večerno z očmi brez solz in nista rekla nobene besede. – (Cankar 1975: 23–24)

Klančar and Noyes: The two old people sat very close together, bent low; and they held each other's hands as they had once held them long years ago; they gazed at the dying sunset with tearless eyes and said nothing. (Cankar 1933/34a: 496)

Thus in example (4) the Past Perfect Tense is used; and in example (5), the last sentence in the sketch, the verb form in repeated and the sentence is reformulated in order to be more in accordance with the grammatical and syntactical rules of English.

It could be then argued that this translation of *Children and Old People* is still Klančar's, but now thoroughly stylistically revised by Noyes. This revision made the text more fluent, natural and grammatically acceptable in the target language. But despite the fact that both Klančar and Noyes were native speakers of English and members of a culture where target-oriented translation was normative (see Venuti 1995), this translation pair nevertheless keeps the original spellings of proper names as sign of cultural otherness in the translation and does not over-domesticate the text.

Conclusion of the analysis

The visibility of nativeness and non-nativeness in translations

In the previous chapter we briefly analysed only those translations (seven in total) that were used in the questionnaire which we shall discuss in the next chapter. The initial study covered 50 translations of Cankar's works which mainly corroborated the findings stated above. Let us sum up and see whether the fact that the translator is a native or a non-native speaker of the target language influences his/her translation strategy, i.e. not only the basic method (either domesticating or foreignizing) adopted by the translator (see Routledge Encyclopedia of Translation Studies 1998: s.v. "strategies of translation"), but also his/her individual and specific translational choices. An attempt shall also be made to ascertain whether the analysed texts support any of the general assumptions regarding inverse and direct translations.

Louis Adamic

Adamic's translation of *A Cup of Coffee* (1922) in many ways supports the claims of those translation theoreticians who are convinced that all non-native translators make unpardonable mistakes in the target language, so that their translations sound foreign and unacceptable to the target audience. However, this early translation by Adamic is not only linguistically weak and unusual, for example even introducing neologisms (e.g. "athrob"), but also reveals a specific approach to translation which allows the translator to freely remodel the text according to his political and literary convictions. Moreover, it seems that the most radical shifts in his translation – which are much more important for the understanding of the sketch than those which are the result of his negligent reading and poor knowledge of English – stem from Adamic's deliberate and conscious remodelling of the text and not from his limited mastery of the target idiom (e.g. the omissions of the Holy Ghost and its replacement with the term "conscience").

His later translations, revealing fewer or no problems with English, exhibit this tendency to change the original texts and attenuate the religious elements in them. For example, in his translation of another sketch by Ivan Cankar entitled *Her Picture* (1926) Adamic omits passages that are more explicitly religious in tone, changes the religious metaphors and secularizes them.

In the same year in 1926 his translation of Cankar's novel *Yerney's Justice* also appeared, first in a left-wing journal of Slovene immigrants in the USA *Prosveta*, then with the new publishing house Vanguard Press in New York. The comparison of those two publications reveals some interesting points: since the publication at Vanguard Press was linguistically revised by the editor, it offers us an insight into the nature of changes necessary to prepare the manuscript for publication. The changes are mainly stylistic, in particular grammatical and lexical collocations are corrected, some minor grammatical mistakes are corrected, the second text has fewer footnotes and fewer Slovene words are retained in the translation. The revisions are not numerous but they almost all fall into the category of collocatability, which might be used in support of Newmark's claim that the greatest problem of non-native translators of the target language is that they do not master collocations in their foreign language.

Despite the fact that Adamic's translations contain many unusual solutions in English, it would be difficult to classify his translations as typical of a non-native speaker. His translations are not faithful to the meaning or the style of the original and at the same time he does not adapt the text to the target culture, since he retains many elements of the original culture unchanged and thus creates opaque, "resistent" translated texts. His translation strategy is specific and consistent: for example, in his translation of the above mentioned *Yerney's Justice* he censors many religious passages (in one instance even replacing the word "God" with "Great Nature", see Kocijančič Pokorn 1999) and creates the work in accordance with his revolutionary political and artistic views. It thus seems that the crucial translational shifts in Adamic's translations are the result of his deliberate remodelling of the text and not of his poor knowledge of the target language.

Agata Zmajić and M. Peters-Roberts

According to bibliographical data, it seems that the Croatian Agata Zmajić and M. Peters-Roberts collaborated only once, i.e. when translating Cankar's *A Cup of Coffee*. Their translation corresponds to the clichéd expectations one has from translators who are not native speakers of the source language since their translation is target-oriented, i.e in accordance with the norm in the target culture, the sentences are redistributed into shorter paragraphs, the punctuation changed, some passages evoking Biblical wording are placed in apostrophes and some poetical metaphors are toned down. However, although both of them were non-native speakers of Slovene, they made only two mistakes which might be attributed to their poor knowledge of the source language.

Jože Paternost

The translation of *A Cup of Coffee* by the Slovene native speaker Jože Paternost is characterised by omissions of translationally more difficult items (e.g. "pred vrata na klanec"), negligent reading or even misunderstandings of the original text (e.g. using "thoughfulness" instead of "thoughtlessness", and comparing the mother carrying the coffee to a mother instead to a child), which is contrary to expectations, since Paternost is a native speaker of Slovene.

In his other translations Paternost also displays his imperfect knowledge of both the source and target languages. For example, in a translation of another sketch by Cankar, *Her Portrait* (1956), Paternost in one case fails to use the irregular form of a verb in the Past Tense and at the same time also does not recognise the literary use of the conjunction "zakaj" (the same mistake Leeming made in his translation), despite the fact that he is a native speaker of Slovene.

As far as his translation strategy is concerned, it is not consistent, even if he publishes in the same newspaper: for example, in his translation of the sketch *Sin* (1957) Paternost attempts to approach the target audience more closely and changes the proper names ("Jože" becomes "Joe", "desetica" ('an Austrian coin worth ten kreutzers') becomes "dime"), but in the sketch *Evening Prayer* he follows the original wording slavishly. In 1958 he combines both strategies when translating the sketch *Holy Communion*. The translation follows the original wording and keeps Slovene proper names, but some of the culture-specific words are replaced by near cultural equivalents in the target language (e.g. "vedomec" (i.e. a person who leaves his body when asleep and becomes an evil spirit) becomes "the Jack o'Lantern").

Translations by Jože Paternost show insufficient knowledge of both the source and target languages, if not also cultures. At first sight, Paternost's translation could be used to support Newmark's claim that translations by non-native speakers are necessarily linguistically deficient, but his translations also reveal poor knowledge of his own native language and culture, which is usually not attributed to native speakers.

Elza Jereb and Alasdair MacKinnon

Elza Jereb and Alasdair MacKinnon collaborated when translating a selection of Cankar's sketches which were then published in Ljubljana by the state publishing house. Their translation of *A Cup of Coffe,* as well as other sketches in this selection, are linguistically and semantically very thoroughly translated. All their translations are source-oriented: they keep the original paragraph divisions, while omissions and expansions of the text are extremely rare, almost non-existent. Slovene geographical and proper names and other culture-specific words are not adapted but are used in their Slovene spelling; if possible, they also try to reproduce the ambiguity and symbolical character of the original. Their translations are at the same time grammatically correct and read fluently; they do not correspond to any of the generalisations concerning native and non-native translators – the translators know the source culture and language well and at the same time master the expression in the target language.

Henry Leeming

Henry Leeming is the only English native speaker in the corpus who decided to translate Cankar into English on his own. His translation of *The Ward of Our Lady of Mercy* reveals certain consistent shifts occurring on different levels of the text. For example, the original long paragraphs and sentences are all shortened; the translation is also marked by numerous omissions: some of them do not affect the understanding of the text, while others change the tone of the whole novel (e.g. the omission of the religious vision at the beginning of Chapter 7). Some of the translation shifts are due to the fact that Leeming read the text as primarily a naturalistic work and thus changed it according to his horizon of understanding. All these shifts can hardly be attributed to the fact that Henry Leeming was a native speaker of the target language.

Leeming translates culture-specific terms literally or uses a more general term in English, and does not replace them with culture-specific terms in the target language. In this case, Leeming acts against expectations: although a native speaker of English he does not try to forcefully domesticate the text.

He does, however, in some, although very rare, instances indicate that he did not understand the source text correctly, especially when encountering archaic or literary use of certain conjunctions – which would correspond to our presupposed expectations.

If we assume that a translator who is a native speaker of a major target language and a non-native speaker of a marginal source language is likely to have poor knowledge of the source language and culture and therefore tends to over-domesticate the text and adapt it to the target culture, then the analysis of the translation *The Ward of Our Lady of Mercy* by Leeming does not support this claim. Contrary to expectations, translational shifts in Leeming's translation are extremely rarely the result of his misunderstanding of the source language. On the other hand, the assumption that Leeming as a competent native speaker of the target language who knows the source language and culture well shall undoubtedly create an "impeccable" translation should also be modified. Leeming's translation of Cankar's novel is in many ways specific: it is characterised by new paragraph divisions, changed punctuation, numerous extensions, changes of meaning and large omissions – and neither the translator nor the editor ever informs the readers that such important changes have been made. Thus *The Ward of Our Lady of Mercy* does not support the claims of the first group of theoreticians who are wary of translators who are non-native speakers of a minor source language and native speakers of a major target language, and it does not support the arguments of those who glorify the work of the native speaker of the target language, since Leeming's translation is predominantly, if not entirely, the result of individual interpretations and translational strategies.

Anthony J. Klančar

Anthony J. Klančar was born and lived all his life in the USA – he was therefore, despite his Slovene parents, put into the category of native speakers of English. He translated numerous works by Cankar, and all of them show the same flaws. In the translation of *Children and Old People* (1933) his English is weak, e.g. Klančar makes some grammatical mistakes, mixes different genres and styles, but at the same time he also does not understand the original well and makes mistakes regarding the meaning of the text. As far as culture-specific terms are concerned, he decides for foreignisation of the text and retains typical Slovene expressions in his translation.

In his translations of other sketches by Cankar *The Captain, The Sun! . . . The Sun! . . .* and *Rue de Nations* (all published in 1933), Klančar again reveals a poor knowledge of both the source and the target languages: he makes some basic grammatical mistakes in the target language (e.g. he uses the conditional in if-clauses and does not use the Present Perfect Tense when appropriate) and in every translation at least once misunderstands the Slovene original – he sometimes misunderstands a word or two, sometimes a whole structure. With culture-specific terms he is inconsistent: some proper names retain the original spelling and diacritical marks (e.g. "Tomaž"), sometimes he omits the diacritic (e.g. "Primoz" instead of the original "Primož"), and then again sometimes he modifies the spelling to assure the right pronunciation (e.g. "Krishtof" instead of the original "Krištof") – and all this in one and the same sketch. He often fails to recognise geographical names (e.g. "Carigrad", which is the Slovene name for Constantinople, is not replaced by the English equivalent in translation; he does not recognise the name of one of the major streets in Vienna "The Ring" and uses "Ringo" in his translation, etc.).

His later translations were even worse; let us mention only the most extreme one, i.e. his translation of the sketch *Her Grave* (1935). The narrator describes the funeral of his mother:

(1)   Prišli smo na pokopališče, da nisem vedel kako in kdaj, nato smo stali kraj globoke črne jame, iz ilovnate prsti izkopane. Pevci so zapeli; kakor iz daljave sem slišal zamolkle moške glasove, besed nisem razumel.
(Cankar 1974:278)

Klančar: We arrived at the cemetery. I knew neither how nor when. We stood beside a deep black hole, dug by hands covered with loam. The singers began their song, I heard low voices of men, as though coming from a distance. I did not understand their language. (Cankar 1935:3)

LT: We arrived at the cemetery, although I did not know how or when, we stood by a deep black pit, dug in clay. The choir started to sing; I heard the men's dull voices from a distance, I could not grasp the words.

In the original, the grave is dug in clay where "prst" (LT: "soil") can also mean "finger" if the gender of the word is changed, but as it is it cannot be understood in the meaning of 'a digit of the hand' in this sentence. This apparent similarity, however, most probably caused Klančar to translate that the hole was dug by hands covered with loam. The narrator tries to convey how deeply hurt he was when he lost his mother, so much so that he could not even understand the songs the choir sang. In Klančar's translation he could not understand their language. This translation thus creates a morbid but also somewhat comical situation: the son stands at the grave of his mother which was dug by hands and listens to funeral songs sung in some foreign language unknown to him.

Translations by A. J. Klančar can thus be either source- or target-oriented: the translator is inconsistent in his choice, sometimes changing strategy even within the same text. His translations reveal, besides a poor knowledge of the source language and culture, which is often associated with translators of central linguistic communities translating a text from a minor linguistic community, also a surprisingly poor knowledge of the target language and therefore do not correspond to presupposed expectations.

Anthony J. Klančar and George R. Noyes

Anthony Klančar was obviously aware of his deficient knowledge of English. He therefore revised some of his translations with the American linguist George R. Noyes and published them in 1933/34 in the London journal *The Slavonic Review*. The revised translation of *Children and Old People* compared to the earlier version by Klančar is more fluent, natural and grammatically correct. The artificial, foreign sounding words are replaced by more neutral ones, grammatical mistakes are corrected. The translation is however revised only stylistically, and mistakes concerning the meaning and understanding of the original are not amended. The translators also in this case decide for the retention of original spelling of proper names and thus keep elements of foreign, source culture in their translation.

The translations of the sketches *The Captain*, *The Sun! ... The Sun! ...* and *Rue des nations* are also revised stylistically and grammatically (e.g. the conditional is no longer found in if-clauses, the correct tenses of the verbs are used) and the texts are made stylistically unified. With all of the texts the original paragraph divisions are retained, except in one, *The Captain*, where the sentences and paragraphs are shortened. But in these translations, too, the mistakes concerning the meaning of the source text are not amended; therefore it seems plausible to claim that Noyes only stylistically revised the translations and was not involved in the process of translation itself. In these translations the spelling of proper names is inconsistent, although not completely following the earlier Klančar version (e.g. the earlier version had "Krishtof", the revised version has "Krištof", but it keeps "Tomaz" and "Buchar" which were used also by Klančar instead of the original "Tomaž" and "Bučar"). The texts are expanded and shortened in the same places as in earlier Klančar versions. Some of the factual mistakes are corrected (e.g. some geographical names are spelled correctly in the revised version), and some are not (e.g. "Carigrad" is changed into "Tzarigrad" and not replaced by "Constantinople", the Viennese Ring is still spelled Ringo).

Translations by Anthony J. Klančar and George R. Noyes are essentially stylistically revised translations by Klančar, since both versions differ primarily in the fact that the revised versions are more fluent and grammatically correct in the target language. The flaws concerning the understanding and meaning of the source text in general remain uncorrected. The texts in both versions attempt to keep some of the specific elements of the source culture, which is manifested in an attempt to retain Slovene proper and geographical names. However, some shifts in these translations also reveal inaccurate knowledge of the source language and culture, which would correspond to stereotypical assumptions concerning the abilities of translators who are members of a central linguistic community and are translating a work from a minor culture.

Native speakership in the analysed translations

The analysis of prose works by Ivan Cankar translated into English more than once does not offer a clear dividing line between the translation strategies used by native speakers and those used by non-native speakers of the target language, where the term translation strategy (see Routledge Encyclopedia of Translation Studies 1998: s.v. "strategies of translation") means not only the basic method (either domesticating or foreignizing) adopted by the translator, but also the specific choices the translator has made in his/her translation. For example Leeming, as a translator from an English-speaking culture who translates the text into his mother tongue, does not domesticate the text and thus follow the normative translation strategy in English-speaking world (see Venuti 1995), nor show inadequate knowledge of the source language and culture. Leeming changes the text according to his interpretation of the novel and transforms the originally impressionistic text into a more naturalistic one, but this change of tone could not be attributed to the fact that he is a native speaker of English. Anthony J. Klančar, despite the fact that he would be granted the status of a native speaker of English, in his translations reveals limited knowledge of both the source and the target languages and creates hybrid texts, in part source- and in part target-oriented. When rewriting some of his translations with the help of another English native speaker, George R. Noyes, he still retains the elements of Slovene culture and revises only the style of the translation. On the other hand, Agata Zmajić and M. Peters-Roberts, despite the fact that they were both non-native speakers of the source language, do not seem to have had problems understanding the text or formulating the target text, which is again against expectations. They do, however, remodel the text radically but retain Slovene proper names.

Nor do translators who translated from their mother tongue into their foreign language correspond completely to Newmark's theoretical assumptions. For example, Louis Adamic, whose translations are primarily source-oriented, in his first translations does commit collocational and grammatical mistakes, but his later translations are influenced primarily by his political and literary views and not by his deficient mastery of English. On the other hand, Jože Paternost, who changes his translation strategy from source- to target-oriented depending on the text at different stages of his translational career, always produces translations that are deficient in English. Moreover, he not only has problems with the target language but also with the source language and often does not understand the original, which is again contrary to expectations. And finally, the translation pair of Elza Jereb and Alasdair MacKinnon – where the directionality would be difficult to define since the translators worked out and into the mother tongue, one of them being a native speaker of the source, the other of the target language – creates source-oriented translations and seems to have problems with neither the source nor the target languages.

This means that none of the stereotypical assumptions on directionality in translation is valid. Almost all of the analysed translators created source-oriented or a mixture of source- and target-oriented translations. Henry Leeming, a representative of a major linguistic community translating from a minor language, would be expected to have problems in understanding the source text and culture, but his translation does not substantiate this claim, since his translation shows satisfactory knowledge of both of them, in fact, superior to some of the native speakers of Slovene included in this study. If we assume that translators who are native speakers of the target language master the use of that target language, then Anthony J. Klančar convinces us that this is not so, since his translations contain numerous grammatical and stylistic flaws and mistakes. If we claim that translators translating from their mother tongue into their foreign language do know the source language and culture but are deficient in mastering the foreign language and culture, Paternost's translations show that a translator can be deficient in mastering both languages involved in the translation process, and that s/he may even have problems with his mother tongue. The only generalisation that can be deduced from the above is that none of the presupposed assumptions is absolutely valid: it is not necessary that the translators from major linguistic communities who translate texts from minor linguistic communities have inadequate knowledge of the source language and culture; on the other hand, it is also not necessarily the case that translators master their mother tongue. Although it is true that translators who are native speakers of the target language more often have problems with understanding the source text and that translators engaged in inverse translation more often create translations that are linguistically deficient, these generalisations are not absolutely valid. Native speakers of the target language can be deficient in their mother tongue (e.g. Anthony J. Klančar) and native speakers of the source language can have problems in understanding the original (e.g. Jože Paternost). It seems that the quality of a translation, its accuracy and acceptability in the target language depend primarily on the individual abilities of the particular translator, his/her translation strategy, his/her knowledge of the source language, culture and the topic discussed, and not on his/her mother tongue or the directionality of translation.

In order to evaluate the results of the textual analysis and at the same time minimise the subjectivity of the conclusions, the general validity of which could be dismissed with the claim that they reflect only an individual's interpretations and assumptions, a questionnaire was designed and administered.

Native speaker intuitions

The questionnaire

The analysis of the translations revealed no particular connection between the mother tongue of the translator and either the quality or the accuracy of his/her translation. However, I needed the help of native speakers of English to test the truth of the final reproach to inverse translation: the assumption that all inverse translations inevitably sound strange to native speakers of the TL, that they contain undefinable elements that are disturbing to native-speaker readers, who represent the text's intended public. This assumption can be found, for example, in the writings of Peter Newmark, who claims that non-native translators of the target language "will be 'caught' every time" (Newmark 1981:180) by native speakers of the TL, and it stems most probably from a widely-accepted hypothesis in linguistics that every native speaker is able to rapidly detect any non-member of his/her linguistic community. For example, Alan Davies in his book *The Native Speaker in Applied Linguistics*, after admitting that there is no consensus among linguists on the definition of the term "native speaker", claims that the detection of non-members of one's native linguistic community is one of the basic and essential characteristics of every native speaker. According to him, every native speaker should have a feeling "of implicit – and very rapid – detection of others as being or not being members" (Davies 1991:94). Thus in order to answer the question as to whether every native speaker is in fact *always* able to immediately detect a non-native translator, and if so, which elements of a text are crucial for such identification, a questionnaire was designed.

Included in the questionnaire were seven fragments taken from four English translations of *A Cup of Coffee*, one translation of *The Ward of Our Lady of Mercy* and two translations of *Children and Old People* (see Appendix I). Two texts were translated by Slovene native speakers: by Louis Adamic and Jože Paternost. Two texts were translated by English native speakers: by Henry Leeming and Anthony J. Klančar. Three texts were translated by pairs of translators: one pair consisted of a native speaker of Slovene and a native speaker of English, Elza Jereb and Alasdair MacKinnon; the second pair consisted of a person who was familiar with Slovene but was not a native speaker and a native speaker of English, Agata Zmajić and M. Peters-Roberts; and the third pair consisted of two native speakers of English, Anthony J. Klančar and George R. Noyes.

The questionnaire was intended for English native speakers only. All subjects were born in an English-speaking community, where they also live and work. They also identified themselves as members of the English-speaking community by indicating that their mother tongue was English. To ensure a homogeneous socio-economic background and competence in English, all subjects were students or staff at different universities. Empirical evidence suggests that not all native speakers are *ipso facto* endowed with an intuitive ability to make judgements about grammar and acceptability. It is assumed, however, that educated native speakers are more reliable, in fact, the more educated the better (see e.g. Paikeday 1984:73). Thus the subjects were all highly-educated native speakers; included in the group were 5 university undergraduates, 8 graduates, 15 masters of arts, and 18 doctors of philosophy, all working in the humanities. There were 46 subjects in total, who varied in age but were all over 20. Since some of the passages were translated by British and other by American translators, 23 subjects were from the UK (11 from the University of Durham, England, 12 from the University of Heriot-Watt, Scotland), 8 from the USA (the University of Kansas) and 15 from Canada (8 from Vanier College in Quebec and 7 from the University of Alberta).

The selected passages in the questionnaire were preceded by a short introduction explaining that the fragments were taken from different translations of two short stories and a novel by Ivan Cankar; that the original texts were written in Slovene, i.e. in a language spoken by approximately 2 million people in Central Europe. The names of the translators were not given, since a foreign-sounding name could influence their answers; however, the date indicating the year when the translation was done was given in brackets at the end of each passage. Subjects were asked to read the passages and indicate whether the translator was a native speaker of American English, British English, some other English (Canadian, Australian, etc.) or some other language, not English. By giving them those options, an attempt was made to inform the subjects that the translators might be members of different English communities. The English native speakers were also asked to briefly describe what their decision was influenced by.

Each translated passage was followed by a question about how many translators were, according to their judgement, involved in the translation. The following three options were given: one, more than one, I could not tell how many. At the end of the questionnaire they were asked to define their "ideal" translation, i.e. they could provide their own definition or decide for one of two options: that the translation should be easy to read and fluent in the TL or that it should be as close to the original as possible, even if the structure of sentences in the TL sounds awkward. Finally, the subjects were asked to specify the translated passage they liked best.

The results showed that even competent native speakers cannot always distinguish between a native and a non-native translator when faced with the translated text only.

Table 1.   Answers given by native speakers identifying the native language of the translators. The third column gives the number of answers indicating that the translator of a particular passage was an English native speaker, the fourth column that the passage was translated by a non-native speaker of English, the fifth column indicates when the subjects could not decide whether the translator was a native or a non-native speaker of English and the sixth column indicates how many interviewees failed to answer the question.

Names of the translator(s)	Mother tongue of the translator(s)	Native speaker	Non-native speaker	Cannot tell	No answer
Adamic	Slovene	20	26	/	/
Zmajić & Peters-Roberts	Croatian and English	35	9	/	2
Paternost	Slovene	14	32	/	/
Jereb & MacKinnon	Slovene and English	31	14	/	1
Leeming	English	34	8	1	3
Klančar	English	9	35	1	1
Klančar & Noyes	English and English	36	7	/	3

Table 2.   Answers given by the interviewed native speakers indicating the native language of the translators, in percentage terms. The language in brackets indicates the mother tongue of the translators.

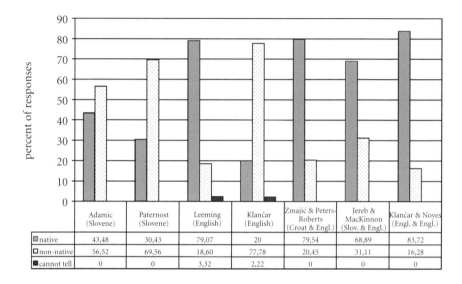

Table 3. Accuracy of the native speakers in identifying the native language of the translators. The third column gives the number of answers correctly identifying the native language of the translator of a particular passage, the fourth column the number of answers incorrectly identifying the native language of the translators, the fifth column indicates when the subjects could not decide whether the translator was a native or a non-native speaker of English and the sixth column indicates how many interviewees failed to answer the question. The bottom row indicates the total number of answers according to the defined categories. Pairs of translators, consisting of a native and a non-native speaker of English, are treated as non-native speakers of English.

Names of the translator(s)	Mother tongue of the translator(s)	Correct answer	Incorrect answer	Cannot tell	No answer
Adamic	Slovene	26	20	/	/
Zmajić & Peters-Roberts	Croatian and English	9	35	/	2
Paternost	Slovene	32	14	/	/
Jereb & MacKinnon	Slovene and English	14	31	/	1
Leeming	English	34	8	1	3
Klančar	English	9	35	1	1
Klančar & Noyes	English and English	36	7	/	3
	TOTAL	160	150	2	10

Table 4.   The results of Table 3, expressed in percentage terms.

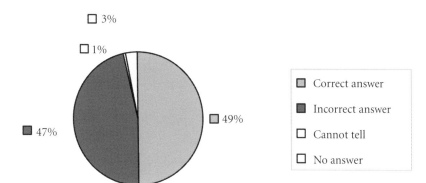

If the two pairs of translators, i.e. Zmajić and Peters-Roberts, Jereb and MacKinnon, each consisting of a native and a non-native speaker of English, are considered as non-native speakers of English, then the percentage of incorrect answers is extremely high (47%). But even if those pairs are excluded from the study, native speakers still prove to be unreliable in defining the linguistic affiliation of the translators.

Table 5.   The accuracy of the interviewed native speakers in identifying the native language of the translators. Pairs of translators, consisting of a native and a non-native speaker of English are excluded.

Names of the translator(s)	Mother tongue of the translator(s)	Correct answer	Incorrect answer	Cannot tell	No answer
Adamic	Slovene	26	20	/	/
Paternost	Slovene	32	14	/	/
Leeming	English	34	8	1	3
Klančar	English	9	35	1	1
Klančar & Noyes	English and English	36	7	/	3
	TOTAL	137	84	2	7

Table 6. The results of Table 5 expressed in percentage terms.

In responding to the passages translated by one translator or a pair of translators consisting of speakers of the same language, a mean of 59% of subjects correctly identified whether the translator of a particular passage was a native or a non-native speaker of English – which is far below the expected rates. 57% and 70% of subjects respectively thought that the two Slovene translators (i.e. Louis Adamic and Jože Paternost) were not English; the fact that 43% of subject still thought that Adamic was a native speaker of English was particularly surprising, since the translator himself admitted that he was still developing his skills in English when he published this translation. The results for the English translators were even more strikingly out of line with expectations: in Leeming's case 79% of subjects thought correctly that the translator's native tongue was English, although 19% of them considered him a non-native, while in Klančar's case only 20% of subjects granted the translator the status of a native speaker of English.

Anthony J. Klančar thus presents a particular problem: according to criteria accepted in linguistics, he should be classified as an English native speaker; however, the response shows that his English would not be accepted as a native variety by other members of the community. And since Davies claims that "The native speaker has a unique capacity to interpret and translate into the L1 of which s/he is a native speaker" (Davies 1991: 149), these results suggest that Klančar was not a native speaker of English after all. His case is even more problematic since the analysis of his translations showed that he had problems with Slovene as well and that he often misunderstood Slovene texts. Would that mean that Klančar was semi-lingual, that his mother tongue was not isomorphic with any language? Perhaps – it does seem to suggest, though, that the number of years of use of a particular language and even the fact that one is born in a particular linguistic community do not correlate with linguistic competence and performance in translation.

Since he was most probably aware of the fact that his English did not sound right to others (or perhaps requested by the journal to stylistically review his translations), Klančar decided to rewrite his translations with Noyes. A passage from that revised translation got a much better response in the questionnaire: 84% of subjects thought it was done by a native speaker of English. In fact, when assessing the passages translated by pairs of translators, a mean of 77% of subjects thought that the passages were translated by native speakers of English (79%, 69%, and 84%).

When indicating the number of translators involved in the translation, the native speakers interviewed were again often in doubt.

Table 7.   Answers given by the interviewed native speakers indicating the number of translators involved in the translation. The third column gives the number of answers indicating that the passage was translated by one translator, the fourth that the passage was translated by more than one translator, the fifth column indicates when the subjects could not decide on the number of translators involved in the translation of a particular passage, and the sixth column indicates how many interviewees failed to answer the question.

Names of the translator(s)	Mother tongue of the translator(s)	One translator	More than one	Cannot tell	No answer
Adamic	Slovene	12	13	19	2
Zmajić & Peters-Roberts	Croatian and English	28	1	14	3
Paternost	Slovene	15	4	22	5
Jereb & MacKinnon	Slovene and English	15	6	23	2
Leeming	English	22	1	17	6
Klančar	English	19	4	15	8
Klančar & Noyes	English and English	18	6	18	4

Table 8.   Answers given by the interviewed native speakers indicating the number of translators involved in the translation in percentage. The language in brackets indicates the mother tongue of the translator(s).

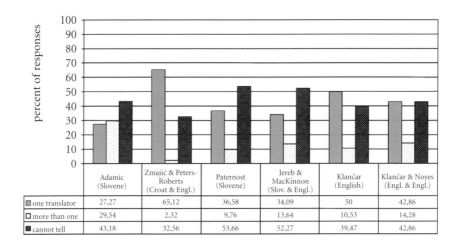

Table 9. Accuracy of the interviewed native speakers in identifying the number of translators involved in the translation. The second column gives the correct indication of the number of translators of a particular passage, the third column gives the number of incorrect answers, the fourth column indicates when the subjects could not decide on the number of translators involved in the translation of a particular passage, and the fifth column indicates how many interviewees failed to answer the question. The bottom row indicates the total of answers according to the defined categories.

Names of the translator(s)	Correct answer	Incorrect answer	Cannot tell	No answer
Adamic	12	13	19	2
Zmajić & Peters-Roberts	1	28	14	3
Paternost	15	4	22	5
Jereb & MacKinnon	6	15	23	2
Leeming	22	1	17	6
Klančar	19	4	15	8
Klančar & Noyes	6	18	18	4
TOTAL	81	83	128	30

Table 10.   The results of Table 9 expressed in percentage terms.

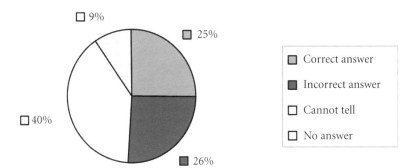

A mean of 40% of subjects were unable to identify the number of trans-lators involved in the translation of a particular passage, and 26% of them made the wrong choice, which means that 66% of 46 subjects interviewed were either unable to tell or were incorrect in identifying how many translators worked on a particular text. The subjects were particularly inaccurate when confronted with collaborative work: a mean of only 10% correctly indicated that a translated passage was the work of a pair of translators.

In accordance with the findings (Venuti 1995), the vast majority of subjects (86%) think that an ideal translation should be fluent and easy to read in the TL. Only 7% of subjects opted for source-oriented translations, and the remaining 7% added that the translator's strategy must be influenced by text type/genre or that the translation technique should fit the target audience.

Despite the fact that some theoreticians argue that translation pairs con-sisting of native and non-native speakers of the target language are "usually an unsatisfactory compromise" (Samuelsson-Brown 1995: 16), the results of this study show the opposite. Surprisingly, translations done by pairs of translators are most appreciated: 83% of subjects chose one of the three translations done by pairs of translators for their personal best, which shows that a collaboration, apparently, does not influence the fluency in the TL.

Table 11. The "ideal" translation strategy according to the interviewed native speakers, expressed in percentage terms.

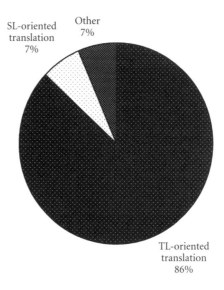

Table 12. The "best" translated passage according to the interviewed native speakers expressed in percentage terms. The language in brackets indicates the mother tongue of the translator(s).

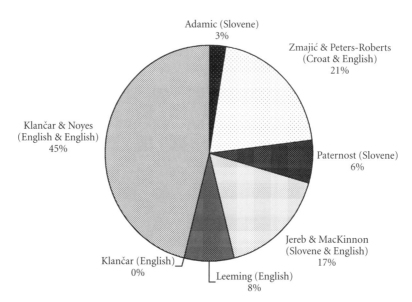

To sum up, the results show that competent native speakers of English cannot *always* locate the foreign and disturbing elements in translations by non-native speakers and that they sometimes find the non-native elements in work by native speakers of the target language. The questionnaire thus shows that the assumption that every native speaker is able to rapidly detect any non-member of his/her linguistic community, when confronted only with a written document, has no solid foundation. Nor can native speakers tell if the work was done by one or more translators. Since native speakers of the TL of the translated text do not find the foreign and disturbing elements in some translations by non-native speakers and the majority of them do not detect such foreign-sounding elements in translations which are the result of a collaboration between a native and a non-native translator, this leads to the conclusion that the definition of the term "native speaker" in linguistics and translation theory is still far from being final and that translation theory should therefore be cautious when referring to the innate capacities of the ideal native speaker. On the other hand, the results of the questionnaire show that translations into a non-mother tongue are often regarded as acceptable by the target readership, with the degree of acceptability depending on the individual capacities of the translator. Moreover, that translations done by pairs of translators are not regarded by the target audience as hybrid and unsatisfactory, but as acceptable as those done by competent native speakers of the target language only.

Conclusion

Does the translator's mother tongue influence his/her translations, and if so, to what extent? Do inverse translations have any typical features that are distinctly different from those of direct translations? Do the results of this study show that some translators are better than others because of their language affiliation?

The survey of different translatological views concerning inverse translation showed that translation into a non-mother tongue is in Western translation theory almost always stigmatised as inferior, despite the fact that the history of translation in the West testifies that inverse translations have been practised from early Antiquity onwards, and that it even has a theoretical grounding in the work of Eugene Nida. It was also argued that the fundamental notions used by the majority of scholars (e.g. the notions of the "native speaker", differences in competence between native and non-native speakers) are undertheorised and possibly also objectively undefinable. Although inverse translation is apparently rare in major linguistic communities, it is often found in minor and peripheral linguistic communities. Since major and central cultures by definition tend to ignore the periphery and at the same time create most theoretical works on translation, the most commonly-found assumption in translation theory is therefore that translators should always translate into their mother tongue. The assumption that direct translations are superior to inverse translations is not supported by any scientific proof and is often ethnocentric: it emphasises the superiority of TL translators, the unattainability of the hidden essence of the target community, a Romantic mystification of language and identification of the nation with the transcendental essence of the language. Since inverse translation has always existed and is still widely practised, translation theory should no longer ignore it.

The analysis of prose works by Ivan Cankar translated more than once into English did not support the generally-accepted assumptions concerning inverse translation. It showed that there are no clear distinctions between the translations by native speakers of English and those by non-native speakers. For example, Henry Leeming, a member of a central and major linguistic community translating from a minor culture, would be expected, according to general expectations, to exhibit in his translation a limited knowledge of the source language and culture. His translation, however, does not support this claim, and testifies to a satisfactory mastery of the Slovene language and culture. With regard to the argument that translators who are native speakers of the target language surely master their mother tongue, i.e. the target language, the case of Anthony J. Klančar proves the opposite, since his translations reveal deficient knowledge of both the source and the target language. In spite of the assumption that translators who translate from one foreign language into another are completely unsuitable for the task, the translation by Agata Zmajić and M. Peters-Roberts, despite the fact that neither of the translators was Slovene, shows no signs of any crucial misunderstanding of the source text or of problems in formation of the target text. Finally, translators creating inverse translations do not completely correspond to the general assumption, since their works are not necessarily linguistically and culturally deficient. For example, while Jože Paternost not only created linguistically and culturally-unacceptable translations in English, he also often did not understand the source text, whereas some late translations by Louis Adamic become more than acceptable. Similarly, pairs of translators defy any simplistic conclusions: while the translations by Jereb and MacKinnon are faithful to the original and fluent in the target language, Klančar and Noyes create translations that are fluent in English but still reveal limited mastery of the source language and, consequently, misunderstandings of the original. The only general conclusion that can be drawn from the study is that none of the generally accepted assumptions is valid. It is not the case that translators who are members of the major linguistic communities, when translating from minor or peripheral languages, do not know the source language and culture well enough; nor is it the case that translators translating out of their mother tongue master the source language but do not know the target language well enough to produce a natural and fluent translation. Although there is no doubt that translators who are native speakers of the target language more often reveal limited mastery of the source language, and that translators translating out of their mother tongue more often create translations that are linguistically and collocationally deficient, these assumptions are not valid in every case and for every translator. Native speakers of the target language can have problems with the target language (e.g. Anthony J. Klančar), and native speakers of the source language may not understand the source text (e.g. Jože Paternost). It seems obvious, then, that the quality of the translation, its accuracy, acceptability and fluency in the target language depend primarily on the individual capacities of the particular translator, on his/her translational strategy, his/her knowledge of the source and target cultures, and not on his/her mother tongue and the directionality of translation.

Finally, the results of the questionnaire designed for native speakers of English showed that competent native speakers of the target language cannot accurately identify, when judging the translated text only, if the work was translated by one or more translators, which means that they also cannot distinguish a foreign voice in those translations carried out by a pair consisting of a non-native and a native translator of the target language (e.g. in our case, Agata Zmajić and Elza Jereb). This represents a serious challenge to the claim that native speakers can inevitably and immediately detect if a particular text was translated by a non-member of their linguistic community, since they obviously cannot distinguish two voices in translations done by pairs of translators.

The results of the question which required native speakers to identify the mother tongue of the translator were similarly inconclusive. Although the majority of subjects found foreign elements in the translations by Adamic and Paternost and felt that Henry Leeming's translation sounds familiar and native, their decisions were not as unanimous as some theoreticians would like us to believe. When assessing the translations by Adamic and Paternost, despite their deficiencies, as many as 43.5% and 30.4% of subjects respectively thought that the translation was done by a native speaker of English; while as many as 20.9% of subjects thought that the translation by Henry Leeming was the work of a non-native speaker of English, or could not decide whether he was a native or a non-native of the target language. Pairs of translators (i.e. Agata Zmajić and M. Peters-Roberts, Elza Jereb and Alasdair MacKinnon) consisting of a native and a non-native speaker of the target language avoid every generalization, since the vast majority of the subjects interviewed (79.5% and 68.9%) thought that their translations were the work of a native speaker of English. The results also show that any kind of arbitrary definition of the notion "native speaker" always proves to be incomplete, since it seems that whether a particular speaker reaches the level of competence in language expected from a native speaker often depends on his/her individual abilities. Thus, for example, the majority of the subjects (77.8%) thought that the translation by Anthony J. Klančar, who was according to the criteria accepted in applied linguistics classified as a native speaker of English, was the work of a non-native speaker of English. Their decision was not influenced by his specific translation strategy since his translation stylistically revised with the help of George Noyes was judged by the majority of the subjects (83.7%) to be the work of a native speaker of English.

The results of the questionnaire refute the claim that native speakers are *always* able to detect whether a text was translated by a native or a non-native speaker of the target language. Particularly unreliable are the judgements of native speakers when they attempt to define the mother tongue of translators who worked in pairs. Not only do they not recognise the collaborative effort of more than one translator, the majority of them also think that the work was done by a native speaker of the target language, despite the fact that the native speaker usually only stylistically revises the translation carried out by a non-native speaker.

Dual authorship also apparently does not influence the fluency of the text in the target language, since despite the fact that the vast majority of the subjects interviewed (86%) first indicated in accordance with the norm in the English-speaking culture that they thought an ideal translation should be target-oriented, the three most popular and appreciated translations according to those same subjects are the work of pairs of translators: the translation by Klančar and Noyes gets 45%, the translation by Zmajić and Peters-Roberts 21% and the translation by Jereb and MacKinnon 17% of the votes.

Some limitations of the study should be mentioned at this juncture – the most prominent being that it deals only with literary texts originating from one culture. Despite the fact that it has been argued in this study that the difference between literary and non-literary texts is blurred, it would be advisable to replicate the study with texts that are traditionally described as non-literary, and created in a different linguistic environment.

However, the theoretical assumptions and empirical data proposed by this study allow us to conclude that the stigma of inappropriateness given to inverse translation by the majority of Western translation theorists stems from a post-Romantic, aprioristic, scientifically-unproven and sometimes ethnocentric conviction of theorists coming from major and central linguistic communities, since inverse translation is mainly practised in peripheral and minor linguistic cultures. Inverse translations do not show any common features, since it is not true that they *necessarily and always* "sound foreign" to native speakers of the target language. In particular, translations done by pairs of translators consisting of native and non-native speakers of the target language evade any simplistic generalisations, since native speakers of the target language usually accept their work as carried out by native speakers of the target language. Translators who are native speakers of the major language and translate from a minor language do not reveal in their translations insufficient knowledge of the source language and culture. Moreover, the status of native speakership does not guarantee that the speaker is also a competent user of his/her mother tongue, since some of the translations (e.g. those by Jože Paternost and Anthony J. Klančar) show insufficient knowledge of the translator's mother tongue. Thus we may conclude that the mother tongue of the translator may or may not influence his creation and that there are no typical features of translations that could be attributed to the mother tongue of the translator. A translation by a native speaker of the target language can be fluent and linguistically impeccable in the target language – but also not. A translation by a native speaker of the source language can be accurate and may reveal the translator's profound knowledge of the source culture – but also not. A translation by a pair of translators can be well accepted in the target language because of its natural style and its accuracy – but also not. It seems that none of the "traditional" and commonly accepted assumptions thus prove to be true and that the translator's mother tongue is not a criterion according to which the quality, acceptability and accuracy of the translation can be assessed. It is therefore also impossible to claim that one particular type of translator is more suitable than another, since the quality of translations done by individuals or pairs of translators primarily depends on the individuals and their abilities and not on whether they are TL or SL native speakers. Thus we may conclude that translation studies should revise some of its assumptions concerning inverse translation, since it seems that acceptability, accuracy and fluency of expression in the target language, knowledge of the source culture and language, and understanding of the source text are primarily dependent on the individual abilities of the translator or pair of translators, on their translation competence and strategy, on their knowledge of the source and the target cultures and languages, and not on their mother tongue or the direction in which they are translating.

Questionnaire

If you feel that any of these questions will identify you in a way you do not wish to be identified, feel free to avoid the answer.

1. Your name (optional):

_____

2. Native language(s):

_____

3. Age: 15–20   20–30   30–40   40–50   50–60   60–

4. Major area of study (specialization):
B.A.: _____
M.A.: _____
Ph.D.: _____

If you are currently preparing for a degree, specify the field and year of study:

_____

_____

5. The following passages are taken from different translations of two short stories and a novel by Ivan Cankar (1876–1918). The original texts were written in Slovene (i.e. the language spoken by approx. 2 million speakers in Central Europe). The date in the brackets indicates the time when the translations were made. Read the passages and answer the questions:

I. One day I craved black coffee. I don't know how it came to my mind; I simply wanted some black coffee. Perhaps because I knew that there was not even a slice of bread in the house, and that much less coffee. Sometimes a person is merciless, cruel. Mother looked at me with her meek, surprised eyes but would not speak. After I informed her that I wanted some black coffee, I returned to the attic to continue my love story, to write how Milan and Breda loved each other, how noble, divine, happy and joyful they were... "Hand in hand, both young and athrob with life, bathed in morning dew-drops, swaying –"

Then I heard light steps on the stairs. It was mother, ascending carefully, carrying a cup of steaming coffee. Now I recall how beautiful she was at that moment. A single ray of sun shone directly onto her eyes through a crack on the wall. A divine light o' heaven, love and goodness were there in her face. Her lips held a smile as those of a child bringing one a gift. But –
"Oh, leave me alone!" I said harshly. "Don't bother me now! I don't want any coffee!" (1926)

– Indicate the translator's presumed native language:
   a) American English
   b) English English
   c) some other English (Scottish, Canadian, Australian, etc.)
   d) some other language, not English

– What was your decision about the translator's native language influenced by? Describe briefly.

_____

_____

_____

– How many translators were involved in the translation?
   a) one   b) more than one   c) I could not tell how many.

II. One day I thought I should like to have some black coffee. I don't know why such an idea came into my head, but I just thought I would ask for some. Perhaps it was that I knew perfectly well there was not even bread in the house, much less coffee.
Lack of imagination can make a man cruel and wicked.
When I asked for a cup of coffee, my mother looked at me with big, shy eyes and made no reply.
Peevishly and grumpily, I left the room, without another word, and went up to my garret, where I wrote of "Milan and Breda who loved each other"; people of rank, happy, and serene, who went "hand in hand, young and gay, through the morning dew and rising sun."
And now I heard soft steps on the stairs. It was my mother, walking slowly and carefully and in her hands was a cup of coffee.
I remember now that she had never seemed to look so lovely. The slanting rays of the setting sun fell through the door of my garret on to her eyes which were big and clear, and as if filled with a heavenly light; love and kindness were reflected in them.

Her lips smiled like those of a child who wants to surprise you with a pretty gift.

But I turned away, and in a cold, cruel voice said, "Leave me in peace; I do not want your coffee." (1933)

– Indicate the translator's presumed native language
   a) American English
   b) English English
   c) some other English (Scottish, Canadian, Australian, etc.)
   d) some other language, not English

– What was your decision about the translator's native language influenced by? Describe briefly.

_____

_____

_____

– How many translators were involved in the translation?
   a) one   b) more than one   c) I could not tell how many.

III. And then, once I craved black coffee. I don't know how it came to my mind; I merely wished to have it. Perhaps it was because I knew there was no bread in the house, not to speak of coffee. A man is in his very thoughtfulness malicious and cruel. Mother looked at me with big, timid eyes and did not answer. Ill-humored and peevish, without a word I returned under the roof in order to write how Milan and Breda loved each other and how they were so happy and gay.

"Hand in hand, together, young, illuminated by the morning sun, washed in the dew..."

I heard quiet steps on the stairs. It was Mother; she was treading slowly and cautiously. In her hand she was carrying a cup of coffee! I recall now that she was never so beautiful as in that moment. Thru the door shone a sloping beam of the noon sun, straight into my mother's eyes; they were bigger, purer, all heavenly light was reflected from them, all heavenly nobleness and love. She smiled as if to a child to whom she was bringing a joyful gift.

Yet I looked around and said in a withering voice: "Leave me in peace! ... I don't want it now!" (1957)

– Indicate the translator's presumed native language
   a) American English
   b) English English

c) some other English (Scottish, Canadian, Australian, etc.)

d) some other language, not English

– What was your decision about the translator's native language influenced by? Describe briefly.

_____

_____

_____

– How many translators were involved in the translation?

a) one   b) more than one   c) I could not tell how many.

IV. Once I felt a strong craving for a cup of coffee. I do not know how this came to my mind; but I wanted it. Perhaps simply because I knew that we had not even bread at home, let alone coffee. Out of pure inadvertence man may be evil and pitiless. My mother looked at me wide-eyed and timid and gave no answer. Sour and full of ill humour, without as much as a word I went up to my loft to write about the love of Milan and Breda, and how noble, fortunate, happy and gay they both were.

"Hand in hand, the two young people, in the full glow of the morning sun, bathed in dew..."

At that moment I heard a quiet step on the stairs. It was my mother; she was treading slowly and carefully; in her hand she carried a cup of coffee. I recall now hat she was never as beautiful as at that moment. Through the door came a shaft of midday sun, right into my mother's eyes. They were larger and purer, all the light of heaven shone out of them, all heaven's love and tenderness. On her lips there was a smile like that of a child bringing a happy gift.

But I turned and said nastily:

"Leave me alone! ... I don't want it now!" (1971)

– Indicate the translator's presumed native language

a) American English

b) English English

c) some other English (Scottish, Canadian, Australian, etc.)

d) some other language, not English

– What was your decision about the translator's native language influenced by? Describe briefly.

_____

_____

_____

– How many translators were involved in the translation?
   a) one   b) more than one   c) I could not tell how many.

V. Her mother got up and kissed her. As her cheeks began to smart with her mother's tears a sudden feeling of tenderness came over her. She raised her hand to touch her mother's face, which was all hot and damp. She saw that face close up before her and it was as if she was seeing it for the first time, broad, flushed and furrowed with tears. The eyes were terrified, swollen, dulled with grief, the lips quivered.
Sister Cecilia led her mother to the door.
"Is she never going to come away from here again?" her mother asked the sister with a strange look in her eyes, like a child begging for a present.
"God's will be done!" Sister Cecilia said quietly. The door closed and the footsteps died away along the corridor. (1968)

– Indicate the translator's presumed native language
   a) American English
   b) English English
   c) some other English (Scottish, Canadian, Australian, etc.)
   d) some other language, not English

– What was your decision about the translator's native language influenced by? Describe briefly.

_____
_____
_____

– How many translators were involved in the translation?
   a) one   b) more than one   c) I could not tell how many.

VI. The children were in the habit of conversing before they went to sleep. They sat for awhile on a broad, flat stove and told each other what happened to occur to them. Evening dusk peeped into the room through dim windows, with its eyes full of dreams; the silent shadows writhed upward from all corners and carried off their extremely wonderful fairly tales.
They related whatever entered their minds, but their thoughts were only of beautiful stories spun out of the sun and its warmth, out of love and hope woven of dreams. All futurity was just one long, splendid holiday; between their Christmas and Easter came no Ash Wednesday. There somewhere behind the variegated curtains silently overflowed all life, twinkling and flashing from

light to light. Their words were half-understood whispers; no story had either a beginning, nor distinct images, no fairy tale an end. Sometime all four children spoke at the same time, and nobody disturbed another; they all gazed fascinated at that wondrously beautiful celestial light, and there every word rang true, there every story had its own pure, living and lucid visage; every tale its splendid end. (1933)

– Indicate the translator's presumed native language
   a) American English
   b) English English
   c) some other English (Scottish, Canadian, Australian, etc.)
   d) some other language, not English

– What was your decision about the translator's native language influenced by? Describe briefly.

_____

_____

_____

– How many translators were involved in the translation?
   a) one   b) more than one   c) I could not tell how many.

VII. The children were in the habit of talking together before they went to sleep. They sat for awhile on a broad, flat stove and told one another whatever happened to occur to them. The evening dusk peered into the room through dim windows, with its eyes full of dreams; the silent shadows writhed upward from every corner and carried away with them their marvellous fairy tales.

The children related whatever entered their minds, but their thoughts were only of beautiful stories spun from the sun and its warmth, from love and hope woven of dreams. All their future was just one long, glorious holiday; between their Christmas and Easter came no Ash Wednesday. Somewhere behind variegated curtains all life silently overflowed, twinkling and flashing from light to light. Their words were half-understood whispers; no story had either a beginning or distinct images; no fairy tale had an end. Sometimes all four children spoke at once, yet no one of them disturbed another; they all gazed fascinated at that wondrously beautiful celestial light, and in that setting every word rang true, every tale had its splendid end. (1934/35)

– Indicate the translator's presumed native language
   a) American English
   b) English English

c) some other English (Scottish, Canadian, Australian, etc.)

d) some other language, not English

– What was your decision about the translator's native language influenced by? Describe briefly.

_____

_____

_____

– How many translators were involved in the translation?

a) one   b) more than one   c) I could not tell how many.

6. According to you, a translation should be:

a) easy to read, fluent in the target language, i.e. in English.

b) as close to the original as possible, even if the structure of sentences in the target language (i.e. English) sounds awkward.

c) other (specify)

_____

_____

_____

7. Which of the translated passages do you like best?

I.   II.   III.   IV.   V.   VI.   VII.

8. If you have any further comments, please provide them overleaf.

Responses in the questionnaire

Legend:

Durham	– the University of Durham, England
Heriot-Watt	– the University of Heriot-Watt, Scotland
Kansas	– the University of Kansas USA
Quebec	– Vanier College in Quebec, Canada
Alberta	– the University of Alberta; Canada
AmE	– American English
EnE	– English English
Not English	– Not English, some other language
OtherE	– other variety of English
?	– I do not know
1 trans.	– 1 translator
More trans.	– more than one translator
/	– the answer was not given

I. Translation by Louis Adamic (1926)

Respondent's no	Respondent's origin	Assumed mother tongue of translators	Assumed no. of translators	Explanation given by the respondent
1.	Durham	AmE	1 trans.	The text seems to be written over-carefully; however, it is perfectly correct in a sort of Ernest Hemingway way.
2.	Durham	EnE	1 trans.	Because of "athrob", "craved".
3.	Durham	Not English	More trans.	A relative unfamiliarity with the language, expressions "that much less coffee", "I craved".
4.	Durham	Not English	More trans.	Not the usual English idioms I am familiar with: "came to my mind", "that much less coffee".
5.	Durham	Not English	?	Line three and five.
6.	Durham	EnE	?	Seems to fit 1920's.
7.	Durham	EnE	1 trans.	A little like reading Barbara Cartland. English, typical of the date.
8.	Durham	Not English	?	Does not read smoothly, it reads like a translation. Second sentence could not have been written by a native English: "that much less coffee", "athrob with life", the use of "divine" and "from heaven" at the same time, the collocation "lips hold a smile".
9.	Durham	Not English	?	Because of "crack on the wall", "and that much less coffee". The whole paragraph doesn't read well.

10.	Durham	Not English	?	Grammatical problems: "that much less coffee", use of punctuation.
11.	Durham	EnE	1 trans.	The use of "mother".
12.	Quebec	Not English	/	The use of punctuation, grammatical errors, the word "crave" seems inappropriate.
13.	Quebec	Not English	1 trans.	It's not smooth. The expressions "and that much less coffee", "loft".
14.	Quebec	Not English	1 trans.	Awkward expressions: "craved", "and that much less coffee", "athrob", "merciless, cruel", "light o'heaven".
15.	Quebec	AmE/OtherE	More trans.	Abrupt style. The expression "o'heaven" sounds Scottish.
16.	Quebec	Not English	1 trans.	Because of "came to my mind", "and that much less coffee".
17.	Quebec	Not English	1 trans.	The translation sounds artificial. This person's English is good but "it came to my mind" sounds foreign.
18.	Quebec	AmE	More trans.	Short sentence structure, words like "attic", "craved".
19.	Quebec	Not English	1 trans.	Phrasing like "and that much less coffee", "divine light o'heaven".
20.	Heriot-Watt	Not English	?	These sentences would not be used in 20th-century English.
21.	Heriot-Watt	Not English	More trans.	Lack of cohesion, lack of coherence, the style is awkward, stilted, lack English turn of phrase.
22.	Heriot-Watt	AmE/EnE	More trans.	Mix of style. Direct, simple style of first-person narrative seems American. Use of "Mother" suggests British rather than American.
23.	Heriot-Watt	Not English	More trans.	Very unidiomatic and sound very foreign.
24.	Heriot-Watt	EnE	?	Use of "Mother" with a capital "M".
25.	Heriot-Watt	AmE	?	Fluent sentence structure, appropriate use of vocabulary.
26.	Heriot-Watt	Not English	?	Idiomatically unusual; "and that much less coffee".
27.	Heriot-Watt	Not English	More trans.	Unidiomatic expression, too formal.
28.	Heriot-Watt	English	More trans.	I suspect this was a native speaker and that the items which sound out of place reflect the date of the translation rather than the origins of the translator. Because of the datedness, however, I cannot be more specific.
29.	Heriot-Watt	Not English	?	Some stilted phrases, the natural flow, the rhythm.
30.	Heriot-Watt	Not English	?	"Oddities" in the language, unnatural English, occasional lack of coherence.
31.	Heriot-Watt	AmE	1 trans.	Not sure – perhaps writing style.
32.	Kansas	AmE	More trans.	Antiquated American English, e.g. "that much less coffee", "athrob", "speak" instead of "say something".
33.	Kansas	EnE	?	The translator certainly has native or near-native command of English. Some expressions "athrob", "light o'Heaven" seem English to me; "that much less coffee" seems like a non-native mistake.
34.	Kansas	AmE	/	"Black coffee" is an American phrase.

35.	Kansas	Not English	?	Expressions: "and that much less coffee", "to write how Milan and Breda", "a divine light o'Heaven".
36.	Kansas	AmE	?	American usage: "to the attic", "leave me alone".
37.	Kansas	OtherE	More trans.	Certain words seem bookish. The stilted clause with "that much less coffee". "Light o'Heaven" sounds Scottish.
38.	Kansas	Not English	?	The phrase "and that much less coffee" is not native English, "attics" are for storage.
39.	Kansas	Not English	?	"Perhaps because I knew that there was not even a slice of bread in the house, and that much less coffee" is odd – one's first inclination is to read "… less than a slice of coffee", which is impossible. "Divine light o'Heaven" is out of place, it is reminiscent of Irish English, but nothing else about the text suggests this coloring. "A single ray of sun" is not native; one would say "sunshine" in native English. The use of tenses is similar to Slovene and lacks English complexity – this could also be a case of someone following too closely the original grammar rather than lack of fluency.
40.	Alberta	OtherE	1 trans.	The phrases "how it came to my mind"; "and that much less coffee", "a divine light o'heaven" are neither American or British English. Still, does not sound as non-native.
41.	Alberta	Not English	More trans.	Some expressions seemed awkward, such as "that much less coffee", "athrob with life".
42.	Alberta	Not English	?	Idioms and tone.
43.	Alberta	Not English	?	The sentence structure is awkward ("that much less coffee"), unusual words ("athrob"), inappropriate prepositions ("crack on the wall").
44.	Alberta	OtherE	More trans.	"that much less coffee", "light o'heaven".
45.	Alberta	Not English	1 trans.	Phrases such as "he lips held a smile as those of a child"; use of apposition rather than subordination or coordination; vocabulary choices, "that much less coffee".
46.	Alberta	EnglishE	?	Use of the word "athrob" and use of the phrase "light o'heaven" seem British to me.

II. Translation by Agata Zmajić in M. Peters-Roberts (1933)

Respondent's no	Respondent's origin	Assumed mother tongue of translators	Assumed no. of translators	Explanation given by the respondent
1.	Durham	Not English	1 trans.	Foreign and un-idiomatic. "Leave me in peace" is unusual.
2.	Durham	AmE	1 trans.	The word "peevish". Generally good idiom.
3.	Durham	EnE	1 trans.	Smoothness suggests a native speaker.
4.	Durham	AmE	1 trans.	Just an impression – nothing specific.
5.	Durham	AmE/OtherE	?	The word "garret".

6.	Durham	AmE	1 trans.	The use of "rank" and "pretty".
7.	Durham	/	?	Journalist style. Possibly English.
8.	Durham	AmE	1 trans.	Slightly formal but "flowery" language reminiscent of American, especially women authors. Clearly produced by a native English speaker.
9.	Durham	EnE	?	The sentences are quite long and flow well – it just sounds English. Also "garret" sounds more English than American.
10.	Durham	AmE	1 trans.	Because of "lack of imagination", "peevishly", "grumpily", the use of "now".
11.	Durham	Not English	1 trans.	"Big, shy eyes" sounds odd, also the use of "garret".
12.	Quebec	EnE	/	Because of "I thought I should like", "peevishly".
13.	Quebec	EnE	/	It has that snobby English sound: "should like to", "peevishly".
14.	Quebec	EnE	1 trans.	Typical English English expressions like "should like to", "peevishly", "garret", "rank".
15.	Quebec	OtherE	1 trans.	English or Canadian, probably Canadian. The loose construction, the absence of contractions.
16.	Quebec	EnE	1 trans.	Expressions "should like to", "I thought I would ask", "people of rank" suggest English.
17.	Quebec	EnE	1 trans.	Because of "I should like". "Lack of imagination can make a man cruel and wicked" makes no sense, so the translator's problem is with the original.
18.	Quebec	EnE	1 trans.	Expressions "I should like to have", "people of rank", "garret".
19.	Quebec	EnE	1 trans.	Fluidity and precision of language.
20.	Heriot-Watt	OtherE	?	This is a much more modern translation.
21.	Heriot-Watt	Not English	More trans.	Style is not cohesive, mainly due to incorrect punctuation.
22.	Heriot-Watt	EnE	1 trans.	Uniformity of style.
23.	Heriot-Watt	English	1 trans.	I cannot define the variant of English because of the date of translation (1933).
24.	Heriot-Watt	/	/	/
25.	Heriot-Watt	Not English	?	Some un-English or incorrect constructions: "I thought I should like to have", "she had never seemed to look so lovely".
26.	Heriot-Watt	English	?	"People of rank" odd in context.
27.	Heriot-Watt	EnE	1 trans.	There are no unidiomatic expressions, except "she had never seemed to look so lovely".
28.	Heriot-Watt	EnE	1 trans.	The translator's confidence to stray from the literal translation of the original is very much that of a native speaker.
29.	Heriot-Watt	Not English	?	The choice of certain vocabulary, e.g. "big, shy eyes".
30.	Heriot-Watt	Not English	?	Sometimes too correct, choice of descriptive words, "went /.../ through the rising sun".
31.	Heriot-Watt	EnE	1 trans.	Reference to "people of rank" and "garret".
32.	Kansas	EnE	1 trans.	Use of words like "garret", "peevishly", the subjunctive tense.

33.	Kansas	Not English	?	Seems too wordy to be a native speaker. It could have been done by a native of English English or some other English but definitely not American English.
34.	Kansas	OtherE	1 trans.	The passage was very clear and flowed as if written by a native speaker, but a few words like "garret" and "I thought I should like to" are not American.
35.	Kansas	EnE	More trans.	Expressions "I should like to have", "I knew perfectly well", "I write of", "peevishly".
36.	Kansas	EnE	?	Expressions "I should like", "garret", "peevishly".
37.	Kansas	EnE	1 trans.	The vocabulary is more appropriate, this has the expected words and structures I mentioned were lacking in the first translation. The style doesn't change throughout the text.
38.	Kansas	Not English	?	Too wordy. The collocaton "an idea comes into one's head" does not sound idiomatic. Translation from a Slavic language.
39.	Kansas	AmE	1 trans.	It is difficult to decide whether this is slightly archaic American English or British English – it could be either. I decided on American because the use of the generic "you"; English English would use "one". I don't know the word "garret" – perhaps it is archaic or British?
40.	Alberta	EnE	1 trans.	Has the ring of interwar British English.
41.	Alberta	EnE	1 trans.	The language use seemed a little stiff, something I usually associate with uppercrust British English.
42.	Alberta	EnE	?	Register does not seem American. Can be some other variety of English as well.
43.	Alberta	EnE	?	The English is correct but old fashioned (I realise it was translated in 1933). My guess is more due to choice of vocabulary.
44.	Alberta	Not English	1 trans.	Phrases are correct but weird: "peevishly", "grumpily", "a child who wants to surprise you with a pretty gift".
45.	Alberta	EnE	?	Vocabulary: "garret", use of "should" in the first sentence, structure of the complex compound sentences.
46.	Alberta	EnE	1 trans.	The phrase "I should like to have some black coffee" sounds distinctly British as does "garret".

III. Translation by Jože Paternost (1957)

Respondent's no	Respondent's origin	Assumed mother tongue of translators	Assumed no. of translators	Explanation given by the respondent
1.	Durham	AmE	1 trans.	"Ill-humored" is American spelling.
2.	Durham	Not English	More trans.	First paragraph seems unidiomatic, e.g. "and then, once I craved", "not to speak of coffee".
3.	Durham	AmE	1 trans.	Could also be a non-native speaker of English.

4.	Durham	Not English	?	When rereding the passage the use of "thru" made me decide to opt for a non-native speaker of English.
5.	Durham	Not English	?	The word "thru".
6.	Durham	OtherE	?	Odd spellings and tone.
7.	Durham	Not English	/	Phrasing and spelling of certain words.
8.	Durham	Not English	More trans.	The use of comma makes the first sentence meaningless. The third sentence reads like a direct translation which has lost its meaning. "Thru" is not a word one would expect from an English native of 1957. Second half is better.
9.	Durham	AmE	?	Sentences sound American, the spelling of the word "thru".
10.	Durham	EnE	?	Formal English: "not to speak of", "Mother", the use of "noble", "withering".
11.	Durham	Not English	?	The use of "thru", the sentence beginning with "a man is in his very thoughtfulness" is rather stilted language.
12.	Quebec	EnE	More trans.	Because of "thru", "peevish".
13.	Quebec	Not English	1 trans.	The expression "I returned under the roof" does not exist in English.
14.	Quebec	Not English	1 trans.	Because of "thoughtfulness", "returned under the roof".
15.	Quebec	Not English	/	The use of "thoughtfulness", "as if to a child" changes the meaning and makes the passage meaningless.
16.	Quebec	AmE	?	The use of exclamation mark in "In her hand she was carrying a cup of coffee!" and "thru".
17.	Quebec	Not English	1 trans.	The expressions "under the roof", "washed in the dew". Artificial.
18.	Quebec	Not English	?	Expressions "not to speak of coffee", "under the roof", "thru", "Mother".
19.	Quebec	Not English	1 trans.	Non-native wording, grammar and spelling errors: "and then, once I craved", "thru", "morn sun".
20.	Heriot-Watt	Not English	?	Some sentences don't seem to be English.
21.	Heriot-Watt	Not English	?	Seems to be some American English influence; punctuation looks a little odd, breaks the flow a touch too frequently, incorrect translation of some words and expressions.
22.	Heriot-Watt	Not English	?	Unconvincing as a text in English, does not read naturally.
23.	Heriot-Watt	Not English	?	A good translation but not a native one. Mistakes: "and then, once I craved", "not to speak of coffee".
24.	Heriot-Watt	AmE	/	Use of "thru" and "ill-humored".
25.	Heriot-Watt	EnE	More trans.	The translator could also be a native speaker of some other variant of English.
26.	Heriot-Watt	Not English	?	Awkwardness.
27.	Heriot-Watt	AmE	?	Stylistically very idiomatic.
28.	Heriot-Watt	Not English	1 trans.	Some of the text does not make sense.
29.	Heriot-Watt	Not English	?	Unusual collocations.

30.	Heriot-Watt	Not English	1 trans.	Clumsy language, problems of register, choice of descriptive words, idiomatic language somewhat "off".
31.	Heriot-Watt	Not English	1 trans.	Some strange expressions and turns of phrase.
32.	Kansas	AmE	1 trans.	Phrase "to speak of", new spelling of "thru".
33.	Kansas	Not English	1 trans.	The syntax is rough. Defintely a non-native speaker of English.
34.	Kansas	Not English	1 trans.	More awkward than a native speaker would be.
35.	Kansas	Not English	?	Expressions "I returned under the roof", "not to speak of coffee", "thru".
36.	Kansas	Not English	/	Awkward: "under the roof in order to write", "thru", "in that moment".
37.	Kansas	Not English	1 trans.	More bookish. I've never heard "under the roof" for "attic". "In his very thoughtfulness" is strange sounding.
38.	Kansas	AmE	?	Spelling of "humor".
39.	Kansas	Not English	/	"Then, once" is strange. The word "thoughtfulness" implies kindness and is illogical in this context. "Thru" has never made into prose style; it belongs to the language of advertising.
40.	Alberta	Not English	?	"Once I craved black coffee", "how it came to my mind", "I returned under the roof", "all heavenly light" sound non-native.
41.	Alberta	Not English	1 trans.	The word order seemed almost Slavic in some instances, as if translated into English almost word for word.
42.	Alberta	EnE/otherE	?	"heavenly nobleness".
43.	Alberta	AmE	?	It is is of a style that I am more familiar with – I assume then that it is American English.
44.	Alberta	Not English	1 trans.	Not always grammatical.
45.	Alberta	Not English	?	Sentence structure; phrasing: "and then, once I ..."; "not to speak of coffee".
46.	Alberta	Not English	?	Some sentences struck me as strange, and not identifiably British, like "and then, once I craved black coffee"; "not to speak of coffee".

IV. Translation by Elza Jereb and Alasdair MacKinnon (1971)

Respondent's no	Respondent's origin	Assumed mother tongue of translators	Assumed no. of translators	Explanation given by the respondent
1.	Durham	EnE	1 trans.	It seems more coherent.
2.	Durham	EnE	?	"Loft" is English, not American.
3.	Durham	AmE/otherE	?	Sophistication in English.
4.	Durham	EnE	?	The spelling of "humoured".
5.	Durham	EnE	?	Seems at ease with the idiomatic phrases.
6.	Durham	EnE	?	Smoothness.
7.	Durham	Not English	1 trans.	Simplicity of language – limited vocabulary.

8.	Durham	AmE	1 trans.	Reads very well. Good short sentences. "Loft" is a very American word.
9.	Durham	AmE	?	Reads smoothly. The phrase "a happy gift" sounds American.
10.	Durham	AmE	1 trans.	"Let alone" sounds American, "midday" could be American, Canadian, or Australian.
11.	Durham	Not English	?	The phrase "happy gift" is odd.
12.	Quebec	AmE	1 trans.	/
13.	Quebec	Not English	1 trans.	Although there are no mistakes, it seems to be a lot of searching for the right phrase. Just an impression.
14.	Quebec	Not English	1 trans.	No mistakes, but there seems to be searching for the right phrase. By 1971 the use of the word "gay" would not be appropriate here.
15.	Quebec	Not English	More trans.	The use of words "inadvertence" and "nastily".
16.	Quebec	Not English	More trans.	Mistakes, syntax, spelling, punctuation.
17.	Quebec	AmE	/	"Bathed in dew" is a native expression; "nastily" sounds artificial.
18.	Quebec	OtherE	1 trans.	Expressions "let alone", "loft".
19.	Quebec	AmE	1 trans.	Phrasing, fluidity.
20.	Heriot-Watt	EnE	?	I like this one the best.
21.	Heriot-Watt	Not English	More trans.	Turn of phrase in not English.
22.	Heriot-Watt	/	?	More convincing than text III.
23.	Heriot-Watt	Not English	More trans.	Mistakes: "I knew we had not even bread at home", "out of pure inadvertence".
24.	Heriot-Watt	OtherE	?	Because of the word "loft" which is not British or American.
25.	Heriot-Watt	Not English	?	Because of "our pure inadvertence", "nastily".
26.	Heriot-Watt	Not English	?	Awkwardness: "they were larger and purer", "we had not even bread at home".
27.	Heriot-Watt	OtherE	?	The expression "loft".
28.	Heriot-Watt	Not English	1 trans.	Certain phrases sound too clumsy: "out of pure inadvertence", "happy gift". On the other hand, some phrases sound very natural, so it could just be a poor translation by a native speaker.
29.	Heriot-Watt	Not English	?	The use of the words "loft", "inadvertence".
30.	Heriot-Watt	Not English	1 trans.	Some word choices are overstrong, it can also be a rough translation with typing errors by a native UK English speaker.
31.	Heriot-Watt	OtherE	?	Don't know.
32.	Kansas	OtherE	More trans.	"Had not even bread" seems neither British nor American. Less rigid use of adverbs than in British English.
33.	Kansas	AmE	?	Syntax and lexicon seem most natural to me. Only "we had not even bread at home" sounds non-native.
34.	Kansas	EnE	1 trans.	This is the most formal translation. The phrases "we had not even bread" and "sour" are English English.
35.	Kansas	Not English	?	Expressions "inadvertence", "loft".
36.	Kansas	OtherE	?	Word choice: "inadvertence", "sour and full of ill humour", "loft", "gay", "I heard a quiet step".

37.	Kansas	AmE	1 trans.	The wording is natural in English. It sounds like I speak, so I'm guessing American English. For example: "let alone coffee", "leave me alone", "craving", "without as much as a word" are phrases I use.
38.	Kansas	EnE	?	The spelling of "humour", the use of "loft".
39.	Kansas	EnE	?	Or maybe some other variant of English. The spelling "humour" precludes American English. It was no longer possible to use the word "gay" to mean "vesel" in 1971, at least in American English.
40.	Alberta	AmE/EnE	?	Could be either.
41.	Alberta	AmE	1 trans.	The language seemed very natural to me. As a Canadian English speaker, I feel this could have been written by an American or Canadian.
42.	Alberta	EnE/otherE	?	I am a native speaker of U.S. English and these versions all sound "stilted" but this might reflect the skill of the translator.
43.	Alberta	EnE	?	Choice of vocabulary: "humour", "pitiless", "inadvertence", "nastily".
44.	Alberta	AmE	/	Familiar casual style.
45.	Alberta	AmE	More trans.	Sentence structure.
46.	Alberta	EnE	1 trans.	The phrase "had not even bread" sounds British, as does the use of the word "inadvertence". The spelling of "humour" also influenced my decision.

V. Translation by Henry Leeming (1968)

Respondent's no	Respondent's origin	Assumed mother tongue of translators	Assumed no. of translators	Explanation given by the respondent
1.	Durham	EnE	1 trans.	It seems coherent to me.
2.	Durham	English	?	Unable to identify any features of a particular version of English – though the good idiom might suggest it is the work of a native speaker.
3.	Durham	/	1 trans.	/
4.	Durham	AmE	?	Overall impression.
5.	Durham	AmE/EnE/OtherE	1 trans.	Can't tell which English.
6.	Durham	OtherE	1 trans.	"Is she never going to come away from here again?" sounds Irish.
7.	Durham	Not English	1 trans.	Reads like translation. Typical of the romantic novel.
8.	Durham	EnE	?	Could really be any English but not likely another language. It reads too well.
9.	Durham	AmE	/	It was a guess. Obviously by English speaker – it reads like piece of English text.

10.	Durham	Not English	/	The expressions are odd: "that face", "she never". Note the errors: "as if she was" (it should be "were"), the wrong use of punctuation.
11.	Durham	EnE	1 trans.	No obvious evidence of non-English English.
12.	Quebec	EnE	1 trans.	The word "smart".
13.	Quebec	AmE/Not English	/	Perhaps it is simply awkward. The word "to smart" is very dictionary.
14.	Quebec	Not English	1 trans.	The word "to smart" is too bookish.
15.	Quebec	AmE	1 trans.	Simple sentence structure.
16.	Quebec	Not English	More trans.	The translator was influenced by Hemingway. American influence.
17.	Quebec	AmE	1 trans.	The unusual use of pronouns.
18.	Quebec	AmE	1 trans.	/
19.	Quebec	AmE	1 trans.	Phrasing "began to smart", fluidity.
20.	Heriot-Watt	EnE	?	All sounds plausible.
21.	Heriot-Watt	EnE	1 trans.	That flows quite well; turn of phrase is good.
22.	Heriot-Watt	EnE	1 trans.	Reads naturally, absence of Americanisms.
23.	Heriot-Watt	AmE/Not English	?	Idioms are all correct. The use of "sister" at that point seems to me very un-English.
24.	Heriot-Watt	/	/	/
25.	Heriot-Watt	EnE	1 trans.	Smooth rhythm.
26.	Heriot-Watt	English	?	I am not very sure whether the translator is really a native speaker of English.
27.	Heriot-Watt	/	?	Couldn't tell.
28.	Heriot-Watt	AmE	?	The use of the word "sister".
29.	Heriot-Watt	Not English	?	Instinct rather than rational thought.
30.	Heriot-Watt	EnE	1 trans.	Nothing "jarred" at a first reading.
31.	Heriot-Watt	OtherE	1 trans.	The phrasing of "her mother asked the sister".
32.	Kansas	OtherE	1 trans.	"Is she never going …" sounds somewhat British, the rest of the text is similar to English.
33.	Kansas	AmE	?	Smooth syntax, colloquial lexical items, e.g. "smart", "all hot and damp", "footsteps died away".
34.	Kansas	OtherE	?	The phrase "smart with her mother's tears" isn't American.
35.	Kansas	AmE/EnE/OtherE	1 trans.	Native English – I can't tell what variety.
36.	Kansas	AmE/EnE	?	Reads well, could be English English.
37.	Kansas	Not English	1 trans.	"Furrowed with tears" is not American English; "the eyes" is not expected, it should be "her eyes"; "come away" should be "leave".
38.	Kansas	AmE/EnE	?	Seems idiomatic and colloquial enough.
39.	Kansas	AmE	?	An American English speaker would have been more likely to omit the conditional "were" in "as if he was/were seeing it" than an English English native speaker.
40.	Alberta	AmE	?	I think "smart" is more likely U.S. English. This is far from certain.
41.	Alberta	Not English	1 trans.	The expression "Is she never going to come away from here again?" did not sound like ti was written by a native English speaker.

42.	Alberta	AmE/EnE/ OtherE	?	Can't say.
43.	Alberta	OtherE/notE	?	There are a few very slight errors that a native speaker would probably not make. Very difficult to pick up.
44.	Alberta	EnE	/	"Is she never going to come away…" – in AmE it would be "ever".
45.	Alberta	OtherE	/	"Come away from here".
46.	Alberta	AmE	1 trans.	No phrases struck me as being particular strange sounding.

VI. Translation by Anthony J. Klančar (1933)

Respondent's no	Respondent's origin	Assumed mother tongue of translators	Assumed no. of translators	Explanation given by the respondent
1.	Durham	EnE	/	It reads a bit like the romantic part of *The Wind in the Willows*.[15]
2.	Durham	Not English	1 trans.	Because of "conversing", "extremely wonderful", "futurity", "visage", "nobody disturbed another".
3.	Durham	Not English	1 trans.	Some words and phrases read awkwardly, not likely from a native speaker.
4.	Durham	Not English	?	Because of "in the habit of conversing", "extremely wonderful", "sometime".
5.	Durham	Not English	1 trans.	Because of "writhed", "visage".
6.	Durham	Not English	1 trans.	It makes sense but is not idiomatic.
7.	Durham	AmE/OtherE	1 trans.	Dated language but possibly English.
8.	Durham	Not English	1 trans.	Quite clearly not written by English speaker. Because of "things happened to occur", "the eyes of evening dusk", "futurity".
9.	Durham	Not English	?	The text doesn't make sense or does not read well. The expression "happened to occur to them" is unusual.
10.	Durham	Not English	More trans.	"Conversing" is too formal. Mistakes in spelling and punctuation.
11.	Durham	Not English	1 trans.	Inappropriate words and phrases: "evening dusk", "extremely wonderful", "futurity", "visage".
12.	Quebec	EnE	/	/
13.	Quebec	Not English	1 trans.	It sounds "bookish", "sometime".
14.	Quebec	Not English	1 trans.	Dictionary translating.
15.	Quebec	Not English	?	The expressions "extremely wonderful", "futurity", "nobody disturbed another", "lucid visage" ring formal to my ears and are not quite natural.
16.	Quebec	Not English	/	Because of "conversing", "happen to occur", "nobody disturbed another".
17.	Quebec	Not English	1 trans.	Because of "conversing", "futurity", "variegated", "silently overflowed all life", "nobody disturbed another", "sometime". The first three expression are too artificial, the rest just non-English.

18.	Quebec	Not English	?	The expressions "sometime", "nobody disturbed another".
19.	Quebec	English/Not English	More trans.	The first paragraph has errors: "stove", "that happened to occur to them"; the second paragraph is very well written.
20.	Heriot-Watt	Not English	?	Not well translated.
21.	Heriot-Watt	Not English	/	The text is awkward and stilted. Turn of phrase not very good, grammatical mistakes.
22.	Heriot-Watt	EnE	1 trans.	Style seems dated and literary.
23.	Heriot-Watt	Not English	?	Idiomatically flawed.
24.	Heriot-Watt	/	/	/
25.	Heriot-Watt	Not English	?	It sounds un-English, maybe this was due to when it was written.
26.	Heriot-Watt	Not English	?	Idioms.
27.	Heriot-Watt	Not English	?	Inconsistent tenor, wrong collocations, unclear anaphoric reference.
28.	Heriot-Watt	Not English	1 trans.	Collocations, clumsy style. Maybe a bad translator.
29.	Heriot-Watt	Not English	?	Too lush.
30.	Heriot-Watt	Not English	1 trans.	Register, word choices, lack of coherence, "over-the-top".
31.	Heriot-Watt	OtherE	More trans.	Gut feeling.
32.	Kansas	Not English	1 trans.	The syntax is really strange, strange lexical items, grammatical errors, "futurity".
33.	Kansas	Not English	1 trans.	Very rough syntax, unnatural word order, "futurity", "converse", rough style.
34.	Kansas	Not English	/	Awkward, words used that wouldn't normally be used.
35.	Kansas	Not English	?	Because of "extremely wonderful", "nobody disturbed another", "futurity", "sometime".
36.	Kansas	Not English	/	Awkward phrases: "conversing", "happened to occur to them", "extremely wonderful fairy tales", "futurity", "nobody disturbed another".
37.	Kansas	Not English	1 trans.	Odd phrases: "happened to occur to them", "futurity", "sometime", "another", "no fairy tale an end".
38.	Kansas	Not English	?	Phrases "futurity", "nobody disturbed another", "living and lucid visage" are not idiomatically English.
39.	Kansas	AmE	1 trans.	Slightly archaic. The word "futurity" strikes me as slightly archaic, but likely contemporary in 1930's English.
40.	Alberta	Not English	?	Unusual word order and phrases (e.g. "nobody disturbed another"; "somewhere behind the variegated curtains silently overflowed all life").
41.	Alberta	Not English	1 trans.	The passage seemed to be written by a non-native speaker using a thesaurus. The word choice is odd in some places.
42.	Alberta	EnE/otherE	?	This version sounds stilted.
43.	Alberta	otherE	?	Obviously done by a native speaker; the use of vocabulary that I am unfamiliar with.
44.	Alberta	Not English	/	Strange word choices: "told each other what happened to occur to them", "extremely wonderful".

| 45. | Alberta | Not English | More trans. | Vocabulary choices: "futurity"; phrasing: "told each other what happened to occur to them", "either-nor", "nobody disturbed another". Structue of complex coumpound sentences. |
| 46. | Alberta | EnE | 1 trans. | Use of the word "futurity" and the particular usage of "holiday" make it sound British. |

VII. Translation by Anthony J. Klančar and George R. Noyes (1933/34)

Res-pon-dent's no	Respon-dent's origin	Assumed mother tongue of translators	Assumed no. of translators	Explanation given by the respondent
1.	Durham	EnE	1 trans.	The same as the previous translation.
2.	Durham	EnE	1 trans.	Good idiom – but unable to describe further why I think this.
3.	Durham	EnE	More trans.	Reads like a native speaker's improvement of translation VI.
4.	Durham	EnE	1 trans.	It was difficult to determine.
5.	Durham	/	?	Can't tell.
6.	Durham	EnE	1 trans.	*Illegible.*
7.	Durham	EnE	1 trans.	A bit flowery.
8.	Durham	Not English	?	As above, because of "eyes of evening dusk", "twinkling and flashing from light to light". Though it is an improvement on passage VI.
9.	Durham	EnE	?	Flows well, no awkwardness of expression.
10.	Durham	AmE	1 trans.	This is an easy read with full expression.
11.	Durham	EnE	1 trans.	No obvious infelicities.
12.	Quebec	AmE	?	/
13.	Quebec	AmE	More trans.	This is a rewording of the translation quoted above.
14.	Quebec	AmE	More trans.	This translator tried to fix the previous translation?
15.	Quebec	EnE	1 trans.	The language is formal but natural.
16.	Quebec	Not English	/	Syntax, "whatever happened to occur to them".
17.	Quebec	Not English	More trans.	"For awhile", "no one of them". This guy read the previous guy.
18.	Quebec	OtherE	1 trans.	Spelling of "marvelous" – probably Canadian.
19.	Quebec	EnE	1 trans.	"Stove" is still a problem.
20.	Heriot-Watt	OtherE	?	Possibly English translation but still some strange lines.
21.	Heriot-Watt	EnE	1 trans.	Flows well, punctuation very good.
22.	Heriot-Watt	EnE	/	Revision of VI.
23.	Heriot-Watt	AmE/OtherE	?	Either American or Canadian.
24.	Heriot-Watt	/	/	/
25.	Heriot-Watt	EnE	?	Smooth rhythm of text.
26.	Heriot-Watt	/	?	Unusual idiom.
27.	Heriot-Watt	Not English	?	Unusual collocations.
28.	Heriot-Watt	EnE	?	The translator coped well with a very flowery text.

29.	Heriot-Watt	Not English	?	Because of "yet no one of them was disturbed".
30.	Heriot-Watt	Not English	1 trans.	The poetic language and metaphors do not quite work.
31.	Heriot-Watt	AmE	?	The "z" in "gazed".
32.	Kansas	AmE	1 trans.	Sounds like contemporary English.
33.	Kansas	AmE	?	Reads smoothly, feels more natural. Images/metaphors seem smoother.
34.	Kansas	AmE	?	Seems to be my native language.
35.	Kansas	AmE	1 trans.	Can't say.
36.	Kansas	AmE	?	Reads well.
37.	Kansas	AmE	1 trans.	It's clear.
38.	Kansas	AmE/EnE	More trans.	Could be either British or American translator.
39.	Kansas	AmE	More trans.	It strikes me as a revision of VI, possibly by a non-native (but competent) speaker. "Marvellous" opens the possibility of English English or other variant of English but this is a spelling that an American, esp. in the 1930's, could have produced.
40.	Alberta	Not English	?	Like passage VI.
41.	Alberta	AmE	1 trans.	This passage again seemed very natural to me, like it was written by an American or a Canadian English speaker.
42.	Alberta	EnE/otherE	More trans.	A bit stilted translation.
43.	Alberta	AmE	?	More familiar – although a Canadian I have read many more American authors.
44.	Alberta	OtherE	/	This is very nice, flowing seamless English. Does not sound American though.
45.	Alberta	EnE	1 trans.	Vocabulary choice.
46.	Alberta	otherE	1 trans.	Spelling of "marvelous" doesn't seem American, but the rest seems similar to my variety of American English, so this represents somewhat of a compromise guess.

Notes

1. The term is taken from the book *Linguistic Imperialism*, in which Robert Phillipson makes a distinction between the core English-speaking countries, like the UK, USA, Canada, Australia and New Zealand, and peripheral English-speaking countries, which require English as an international link language (e.g. Japan, Slovenia; also known as EFL, or English as a Foreign Language countries), and countries on which English was imposed in colonial times (e.g. India, Nigeria; also known as ESL, or English as a Second Language countries) (Phillipson 1992:17).

2. Similarly vague is the term "non-native speaker". Some researchers (for example, William D. Davies & Tamar I. Kaplan 1998) use the term "non-native speaker" for learners of a foreign language and exclude all those non-native speakers who do not learn the language in language classes but are immersed in the new linguistic community, for example immigrants. The results of such studies, for example on the grammaticality judgements of L2 learners, are not valid for all non-native speakers, but only for those who learned the foreign language in classrooms.

3. David Crystal adds that here Chomsky focusses on syntax and phonology only and ignores vocabulary development, which never concludes in childhood (Crystal in Paikeday 1985:71).

4. "Since languages express cultures, translators should be bicultural, not bilingual" (Lefevere & Bassnett 1990:11).

5. "Seine [a translator's] erste Regel muß sein, sich wegen des Verhältnisses, in dem seine Arbeit zu einer *fremden Sprache* steht, nichts zu erlauben was nicht auch jeder ursprünglichen Schrift gleicher Gattung in der *heimlichen Sprache* erlaubt wird" (Schleiermacher 1985:322; emphasis added).

6. "The poet translator creates the main source of influence, which is the text he or she creates *in his or her own language*" (Barnstone 1993:109; emphasis added).

7. "Through the foreign language we renew our love-hate intimacy with our mother tongue" (Johnson 1985:142).

8. "Translation plays out in the open the 'everyday frustrations' of writing, projecting them into an external form. We transfer our frustrations to the mother tongue [...]" (Simon 1996:94).

9. "Some of the most persuasive translations in the history of the metier have been made by writers ignorant of the language from which they were translating (this would be so notably where rare, "exotic" languages are involved)" (Steiner 1992:375).

10. The first one to use the word in that sense was Eugen Wolff in 1886.

11. There exists also a manuscript version by Anthony Klančar, entitled *House of Our Lady of Mercy*. But since in this study translations are defined functionally, i.e. as texts presented or regarded as translations within the target culture (see Toury 1980: 37, 43–45, 1985: 20, 1995: 32), then manuscripts with which a target audience did not come into contact fall outside the definition [and are thus excluded from consideration].

12. Cankar wrote to his cousin: "One passage I would not have written again, it is unnecessary and ambiguous. That is why I prohibited those pages in the Russian and Czech translations. But let those pages stay in Slovene! Because Slovene flag-wavers, tail-coated philistines and hackney drivers are eager for scandal, let them have it then!" (Iz. Cankar 1960: 9–10).

13. All emphases are mine.

14. All literal translations are mine.

15. By Kenneth Grahame (1859–1932), first published in 1908.

Bibliography

Adamič, L. (1934). "What the proletariat reads: Conclusions based upon a year's study among hundreds of workers throughout the United States." *The Saturday Review of Literature, 20* (December), 321–322.

Aristeas to Philocrates (1997) (130 B.C). Transl. by Moses Hadas. In Douglas Robinson (Ed.), *Western Translation Theory: From Herodotus to Nietzsche* (pp. 4–6). Manchester: St. Jerome Publishing.

Barnstone, W. (1993). *The Poetics of Translation: History, Theory, Practice.* New Haven, London: Yale University Press.

Beeby Lonsdale, A. (1998). "Direction of translation: Directionality." In Mona Baker (Ed.), *Routledge Encyclopedia of Translation Studies* (pp. 63–67). London, New York: Routledge.

Bele, V. (1909). "Cankar in Biblija." *Čas, 3,* 349–374.

Bell, Roger T. (1991). *Translation and Translating.* London, New York: Longman.

Benjamin, W. (1982). "The Task of the Translator". In H. Arendt (Ed.), Walter Benjamin, *Illuminations* (pp. 69–82). London: Fontana.

Bernik, F. (1969). "Cankarjevi prvi nastopi v javnosti in literarna kritika." *Slavistična revija, 17,* 13–23.

Bernik, F. (1971). "Problem fabule v zgodnjem pripovedništvu Ivana Cankarja." *VII. seminar slovenskega jezika, literature in kulture* (pp. 283–297). Ljubljana: Univerza v Ljubljani, Filozofska fakulteta, Oddelek za slovanske jezike in književnosti.

Bernik, F. (1976). "Cankarjeva avtobiografska proza." *XII. seminar slovenskega jezika, literature in kulture* (pp. 73–87). Ljubljana: Univerza v Ljubljani, Filozofska fakulteta, Oddelek za slovanske jezike in književnosti.

Bernik, F. (1976). "Inovativnost Cankarjeve vinjetne proze." *Slavistična revija, 24,* 237–265.

Bernik, F. (1977). "Simbolizem v Cankarjevi prozi." *XIII. seminar slovenskega jezika, literature in kulture* (pp. 69–80). Ljubljana: Univerza v Ljubljani, Filozofska fakulteta, Oddelek za slovanske jezike in književnosti.

Bernik, F. (1977). "Uvod v problematiko Cankarjevega romana." In J. Vidmar, Š. Barbarič, & F. Zadravec (Eds.), *Simpozij o Ivanu Cankarju 1976* (pp. 252–258). Ljubljana: Slovenska matica.

Bernik, F. (1981). "Cankarjevo upanje v Podobah iz sanj." In Ivan Cankar (Ed.), *Podobe iz sanj* [Zbirka Kondor 197]. Ljubljana: Mladinska knjiga.

Bernik, F. (1983a). "Slogovne tendence Cankarjeve črtice." *Slavistična revija, 31,* 269–279.

Bernik, F. (1983b). *Tipologija Cankarjeve proze.* Ljubljana: Cankarjeva založba.

Bernik, F. (1985a). "Simbolizem v slovenski književnosti." *XXI. seminar slovenskega jezika, literature in kulture* (pp. 155–169). Ljubljana: Univerza v Ljubljani, Filozofska fakulteta, Oddelek za slovanske jezike in književnosti.

Bernik, F. (1985b). "Uporništvo in resignacija v socialni pripovedi." In Ivan Cankar (Ed.), *Dela 3*. Ljubljana: Cankarjeva založba.

Bernik, F. (1987). *Ivan Cankar: Monografska študija*. Ljubljana: Državna založba Slovenije.

Bernik, F. (1988). "The Introduction of Symbolism to Slovene Literature." *Slovene Studies, 10*, 161–169.

Bernik, F. (1993). "Književnost slovenske moderne v evropskem kontekstu." *Slavistična revija, 41*, 13–23.

Bernik, F. (1994). "Položaj distance v Cankarjevi pripovedni tehniki." *Individualni in generacijski ustvarjalni ritmi v slovenskem jeziku, književnosti in kulturi* (pp. 381–386). Ljubljana: Univerza v Ljubljani, Filozofska fakulteta, Oddelek za slovanske jezike in književnosti.

Bernik, F. (1996). "Od dekadence k angažirani umetnosti in simbolizmu." *Nova revija, 15* (Ampak), 7–9.

Bialystok, Ellen (1998). "Coming of Age in Applied Linguistics." *Language Learning, 48* 4 (December), 497–518.

Birdsong, D. (1992). "Ultimate attainment in second language acquisition." *Language, 68*, 706–755.

Bley-Vroman, R. (1990). "The Logical Problem of Foreign Language Learning." *Linguistic Analysis, 20* (1–2), 3–49.

Bongaerts, T., B. Planken, E. Schils (1995). "Can late starters attain a native accent in a foreign language: A test of the critical period hypothesis." In David Singleton & Z. Lengyel (Eds.), *The Age Factor in Second Language Acquisition* (pp. 30–50). Clevedon: Multilingual Matters.

Breznik, A. (1935). "Jezik naših pripovednikov." *Dom in svet, 48*, 505–510.

Bussmann, H. (Ed.). (1996). *Routledge Dictionary of Language and Linguistics*. London, New York: Routledge.

Campbell, S. (1998). *Translation into the Second Language*. London, New York: Longman.

Canagarajah, Suresh A. (1999). "On EFL Teachers, awareness and agency." *ELT Journal, 53* 3 (July), 207–214.

Cankar, I. (1926). "A Cup of Coffee." Trans. by Louis Adamic. *Juvenile – Mladinski list, 5*, 82–83.

Cankar, Ivan (1926). "Her Picture." Trans. by Louis Adamic. *Juvenile – Mladinski list, 5* (6), 176–177.

Cankar, Ivan (1926). *Yerney's Justice*. Trans. by Louis Adamic. *Prosveta, 19* (19. May, 6).

Cankar, Ivan (1926). *Yerney's Justice*. Trans. by Louis Adamic. *Prosveta, 19* (26. May, 6).

Cankar, Ivan (1926). *Yerney's Justice*. Trans. by Louis Adamic. *Prosveta 19* (2. June, 6).

Cankar, Ivan (1926). *Yerney's Justice*. Trans. by Louis Adamic. *Prosveta, 19* (9. June, 6).

Cankar, Ivan (1926). *Yerney's Justice*. Trans. by Louis Adamic. *Prosveta, 19* (16. June, 6).

Cankar, Ivan (1926). *Yerney's Justice*. Trans. by Louis Adamic. *Prosveta, 19* (23. June, 6).

Cankar, Ivan (1926). *Yerney's Justice*. Trans. by Louis Adamic. *Prosveta, 19* (30. June, 6).

Cankar, Ivan (1926). *Yerney's Justice*. Trans. by Louis Adamic. *Prosveta, 19* (7. July, 6).

Cankar, Ivan (1926). *Yerney's Justice*. Trans. by Louis Adamic. *Prosveta, 19* (14. July, 6).

Cankar, Ivan (1926). *Yerney's Justice*. Trans. by Louis Adamic. *Prosveta, 19* (21. July, 6).

Cankar, Ivan (1926). *Yerney's Justice*. Trans. by Louis Adamic. *Prosveta, 19* (28. July, 6).

Cankar, Ivan (1926). *Yerney's Justice*. Trans. by Louis Adamic. *Prosveta, 19* (4. Aug., 6).

Cankar, Ivan (1926). *Yerney's Justice*. Trans. by Louis Adamic. *Prosveta, 19* (11. Aug., 6).

Cankar, Ivan (1926). *Yerney's Justice*. Trans. by Louis Adamic. *Prosveta, 19* (18. Aug., 6).

Cankar, Ivan (1926). *Yerney's Justice*. Trans. by Louis Adamic. *Prosveta, 19* (25. Aug., 6).

Cankar, Ivan (1926). *Yerney's Justice*. Trans. by Louis Adamic. *Prosveta, 19* (1. Sept., 6).

Cankar, Ivan (1926). *Yerney's Justice*. Trans. by Louis Adamic. *Prosveta, 19* (8. Sept., 6).

Cankar, Ivan (1926). *Yerney's Justice*. Trans. by Louis Adamic. *Prosveta, 19* (15. Sept., 6).

Cankar, Ivan (1926). *Yerney's Justice*. Transl. and introduction by Louis Adamic. New York: Vanguard Press.

Cankar, Ivan (1933). "Children and Old People." Trans. by Anthony J. Klančar. *New Era – Nova doba, 9* (36), 6.

Cankar, Ivan (1933). "Cup of Coffee." Trans. by Agata Zmajić & M. Peters-Roberts. *Review of Reviews, 84* (1), 52–53.

Cankar, Ivan (1933). "Rue des nations." Trans. by Anthony J. Klančar. *New Era – Nova doba, 9* (33), 6.

Cankar, Ivan (1933). "The Captain." Trans. by Anthony J. Klančar. *New Era – Nova doba, 9* (20. September, 37), 6.

Cankar, Ivan (1933). "The sun! ... The sun!" Trans. by Anthony J. Klančar. *New Era – Nova doba, 9* (24), 6.

Cankar, Ivan (1933). "Rue des nations." Trans. by Anthony J. Klančar. *New Era – Nova doba, 9* (33), 6.

Cankar, Ivan (1934/35). "Children and Old People." Trans. by Anthony J. Klančar & George R. Noyes. *The Slavonic Review, 13,* 494–496.

Cankar, Ivan (1934/35). "The Captain." Trans. by Anthony J. Klančar & George R. Noyes. *The Slavonic Review, 13,* 496–498.

Cankar, Ivan (1934/35). "The Sun! ... The Sun!" Trans. by Anthony J. Klančar & George R. Noyes. *The Slavonic Review, 13,* 498–501.

Cankar, Ivan (1934/35). "Rue des nations." Trans. by Anthony J. Klančar & George R. Noyes. *The Slavonic Review, 13,* 503–506.

Cankar, Ivan (1935). "Her Grave." Trans. by Anthony J. Klančar. *Skyline, 7* (3), 3–5.

Cankar, Ivan (1956). "Her Portrait." Trans. by Jože Paternost. *Ameriška domovina* (28. Dec., 6).

Cankar, Ivan (1957). "A Cup of Coffee." Trans. by Jože Paternost. *Ameriška domovina* (8. February, 6).

Cankar, Ivan (1957). "Evening Prayer." Trans. by Jože Paternost. *Ameriška domovina* (8. March, 6).

Cankar, Ivan (1957). "Sin." Trans. by Jože Paternost. *Ameriška domovina* (1. Feb., 6).

Cankar, Ivan (1958). "Holy Communion." Trans. by Jože Paternost. *Ameriška domovina* (21. March, 6).

Cankar, I. (1971). "A Cup of Coffee." *My Life and Other Sketches*. Trans. by Elza Jereb, Alasdair MacKinnon. Ljubljana: Državna založba Slovenije.

Cankar, I. (1971). *Zbrano delo*. Zbrana dela slovenskih pesnikov in pisateljev 10. Ljubljana: Državna založba Slovenije.

Cankar, I. (1971). *Zbrano delo*. Zbrana dela slovenskih pesnikov in pisateljev 27. *Pisma* II. Ljubljana: Državna založba Slovenije.

Cankar, I. (1972). *Zbrano delo*. Zbrana dela slovenskih pesnikov in pisateljev 11. *Hiša Marije Pomočnice. Mimo življenja*. Ljubljana: Državna založba Slovenije.

Cankar, I. (1972). *Zbrano delo*. Zbrana dela slovenskih pesnikov in pisateljev 28. *Pisma* III. Ljubljana: Državna založba Slovenije.

Cankar, I. (1975). *Zbrano delo*. Zbrana dela slovenskih pesnikov in pisateljev 22. Ljubljana: Državna založba Slovenije.

Cankar, I. (1975). *Zbrano delo*. Zbrana dela slovenskih pesnikov in pisateljev 23. *Podobe iz sanj. Črtice 1915–1918*. Ljubljana: Državna založba Slovenije.

Cankar, I. (1976). *The Ward of Our Lady of Mercy*. Trans. by Henry Leeming in 1968. Ljubljana: Državna založba Slovenije.

Cankar, I. (1976). *Zbrano delo*. Zbrana dela slovenskih pesnikov in pisateljev 30. *Pisma* V. Ljubljana: Državna založba Slovenije.

Cankar, Izidor (1920). "Ivan Cankar v Zadrugi." *Dom in svet, 33*, 12–17.

Cankar, Izidor (1926). "Govor ob petdesetletnici rojstva Ivana Cankarja." *Dom in svet*, 365–372.

Cankar, Izidor (1930). *Zbrani spisi* 11. Ljubljana: Nova založba.

Cankar, Izidor (1960). *Obiski* [Knjižnica Kondor 39]. Ljubljana: Mladinska knjiga.

Cankar, Izidor (1969). *Leposlovje – Eseji, kritika*. Ljubljana: Slovenska matica.

Cao, D. (1996). "Towards a Model of Translation Proficiency." *Target, 8* (2), 325–340.

Catford, J. C. (1965). *A Linguistic Theory of Translation*. Oxford: Oxford University Press.

Chomsky, N. (1965). *Aspects of the Theory of Syntax*. Cambridge MA: MIT Press.

Christian, Henry A. (1978). "Adamičevi prevodi in izbor jugoslovanskih zgodb." *Zbornik občine Grosuplje, 10*, 215–230.

Chu Chi, Yu (2000). "Translation Theory in Chinese Translations of Buddhist Texts." In Beeby, Allison, Doris Ensinger, & Marisa Presas (Eds.), *Investigating Translation* (pp. 43–53). Amsterdam, Philadelphia: John Benjamins.

Cook, V. (1991). *Second Language Learning and Language Teaching*. London, New York, Sydney, Aukland: Arnold.

Cook, Vivian (1999). "Going Beyond the Native Speaker in Language Teaching." *TESOL Quarterly, 33* 2 (Summer), 185–209.

Coppieters, R. (1987). "Competence Differences Between Native and Near-Native Speakers." *Language, 63* (3), 544–573.

Crystal, D. (1992). *Introducing Linguistics*. London, New York, Ringwood, Toronto, Aukland: Penguin Group.

Crystal, D. (1994 [1987]). *The Cambridge Encyclopedia of Language*. Cambridge, New York, Melbourne: Cambridge University Press.

Cvetek-Russi, L. (1977). "Jezik in slog v Cankarjevem proznem ustvarjanju." Simpozij o Ivanu Cankarju na tržaški univerzi. *Sodobnost, 25*, 752–754.

D. S. (1904). "Ivan Cankar: *Hiša Marije Pomočnice*." *Dom in svet, 17*, 308.

Davies, A. (1991). *The Native Speaker in Applied Linguistics*. Edinburgh: Edinburgh University Press.

Davies, Alan (1996). "Proficiency or the native speaker: What are we trying to achieve in ELT?" In G. Cook & B. Seidhofer (Eds.), *Principle and practice in applied linguistics* (pp. 145–157). Oxford: Oxford University Press.

Davies, Alan (2003). *The Native Speaker: Myth and Reality*. Clevedon, Buffalo, Toronto, Sydney: Multilingual Matters.

Davies, W. D., & Tamar I. Kaplan (1998). "Native Speaker vs. L2 learner grammaticality judgements." *Applied Linguistics, 19* (2), 183–201.

Debevec, J. (1918). "Dom in svet, letnik 1917." *Jugoslovan, 16* (februar), 1–2.

Delille, J. (1992). "Preface to his translation of Virgil's *Georgics*. In A. Lefevere (Ed.), *Translation/History/Culture: A Sourcebook* (pp. 37–38). London, New York: Routledge.

Doorslaer, Luc van (1995). "Quantitative and Qualitative Aspects of Corpus Selection in Translation Studies." *Target, 7* (2), 245–260.

Dryden, J. (1997 [1680]). "The Three Types of Translation." From "Preface" to Ovid's *Epistles* (1680). In Douglas Robinson (Ed.), *Western Translation Theory: From Herodotus to Nietzsche* (pp. 171–175). Manchester: St. Jerome Publishing.

Duarte, Edward (King of Portugal) (1997 [1430s]). "The Art of Translating from Latin." From The Loyal Counselor. In Douglas Robinson (Ed.), *Western Translation Theory: From Herodotus to Nietzsche* (p. 60). Manchester: St. Jerome Publishing.

Duff, A. (1981). *The Third Language: Recurrent Problems of Translation into English*. Oxford, New York, Toronto, Sydney, Paris, Frankfurt: Pergamon Press.

Duff, A. (1989). *Translation*. Oxford: Oxford University Press.

Dulay, H., Marina Burt, Stephen Krashen (1982). *Language two*. New York, Oxford: Oxford University Press.

Eagleton, T. (1983). *Literary Theory: An Introduction*. Minneapolis: University of Minnesota Press.

Eisenstein, M., & Jean W. Bodman (1986). " 'I very appreciate!': expressions of gratitude by native and non-native speakers of American English." *Applied Linguistics, 7* (2), 167–185.

Enciklopedija Slovenije (1987–). Marjan Javornik (Ed.). Ljubljana: Mladinska knjiga.

Faulkner Larry R., & John R. Durbin (2000). "In Memoriam. Andre Lefevere." www.utexas.edu/faculty/council/1998–1999/ memorials/Lefevere/lefevere.htm

Gangl, E. (1918). "Književnost: *Podobe iz sanj.*" *Učiteljski tovariš, 22* (Feb), 5.

Glonar, J. A. (1918). "Ivan Cankar: *Podobe iz sanj.*" *Ljubljanski zvon, 38,* 146–147.

Golar, C. (1903/1904). "Ivan Cankar: *Hiša Marije Pomočnice.*" *Slovan, 2,* 187–188.

Grosjean, F. (1982). *Life With Two Languages: An Introduction to Bilingualism*. Cambridge, Mass.: Harvard University Press.

Grosman, M., Mira Kadrić, Irena Kovačič, & Mary Snell-Hornby (Eds.). (2000). *Translation into Non-Mother Tongues: In Professional Practice and Training*. Tübingen: Stauffenburg (Studien zur Translation 8).

Gspan, A. (1936). "Ivan Cankar: Zbrani spisi XVIII." *Ljubljanski zvon, 56,* 98–102.

Gutt, E.-A. (1990). "A Theoretical Account of Translation – Without a Translation Theory." *Target, 2* (2), 135–164.

Harvard Encyclopedia of American Ethnic Groups (1980). Stephan Thernstrom (Ed.). Cambridge MA, London: Harvard University Press.

Herder, J. G. (1977). Fragmente. In *Translating literature: The German Tradition: From Luther to Rosenzweig* [Approaches to Translation Studies 4], A. Lefevere (Ed.). Assen, Amsterdam: Van Gorcum.

Hribar, T. (1983). *Drama hrepenenja: Od Cankarjeve do Šeligove Lepe Vide.* Ljubljana: Mladinska knjiga.

Hugo, V. (1992). "Introduction to the translation of Shakespeare." In A. Lefevere (Ed.), *Translation/History/Culture: A Sourcebook, 18.* London, New York: Routledge.

Humboldt, W. von (1977). "Einleitung to Aeschylos' Agamemnon metrisch übersetzt von Wilhelm von Humboldt." In A. Lefevere (Ed.), *Translating literature: The German Tradition: From Luther to Rosenzweig* [Approaches to Translation Studies 4] (pp. 40–45). Assen, Amsterdam: Van Gorcum.

Humboldt, Wilhelm von (1997). "The More Faithful, The More Divergent. From the introduction to his translation of Aeschylus' Agamemnon (1816)." In Douglas Robinson (Ed.), *Western Translation Theory: From Herodotus to Nietzsche* (pp. 239–240). Manchester: St. Jerome Publishing.

Ilešič, F. (1917). "Literarni pregled." *Slovenski narod, 31* (december), 1–2.

Ioup, Georgette, Elizabeth Boustagui, Manal El Tigi, & Martha Moselle. (1994). "Reexamining the Critical Period Hypothesis: A Case Study of Successful Adult SLA in a Naturalistic Environment." *Studies in Second Language Acquisition, 16,* 73–98.

Ivan Cankar v prevodih, [Zbornik društva književnih prevajalcev Slovenije] (1977). Murska Sobota: Pomurska založba.

Johnson, B. (1985). "Taking Fidelity Philosophically." In J. Graham (Ed.), *Difference in Translation* (pp. 142–148). New York: Cornell University Press.

Kachru, Braj B. (1991). "Liberation linguistics and the Quirk Concern." *English Today, 25* (1), 3–13.

Kelly, D. (Ed.). (2003). *La direccionalidad en traducción e interpretación : Perspectivas teóricas, profesionales y didácticas.* Granada: Editorial Atrio.

Kelly, L. G. (1979). *The True Interpreter: A History of Translation Theory and Practice in the West.* Oxford: Basil Blackwell.

Kermauner, T. (1974). Introduction to *Hiša Marije Pomočnice* Ivana Cankarja. Ljubljana: Mladinska knjiga.

Kim, K. H. S., N. R. Relkin, L. Kyoung-Min, & J. Hirsch (1997). "Distinct cortical areas associated with native and second languages." *Nature, 388,* 171–174.

Klančar, A. J. (1938). "Cankar v angleščini." *Cankarjev glasnik, 2* (December), 127–130.

Kobal, F. (1904). "Ivan Cankar: *Hiša Marije Pomočnice.*" *Slovenski narod, 30* (April–4 May).

Koblar, F. (1920). "Ivan Cankar: Moje življenje." *Dom in svet, 33,* 139.

Koblar, F. (1926). "Ivan Cankar: Zbrani spisi I–III." *Dom in svet, 39* 189–191.

Kocijančič Pokorn, N. (1999). "A Slovene Classic in Translation: Usurpation or a Legitimate Political Translation?" In Jeroen Vandaele (Ed.), *Translation and the (Re)location of Meaning* (pp. 195–214). Leuven: CETRA.

Kocijančič, G. (2004). "O anarhizmu." In *Tistim zunaj. Eksoterični zapisi 1990–2003* (pp. 57–60). Ljubljana: Kud Logos.

Kocijančič, N. (1993). "On Louis Adamic's translation of Cankar´s *Hlapec Jernej in njegova pravica.*" *Slovene Studies: Journal of Slovene Studies in Canada, 15* (1–2), 139–150.

Kos, J. (1982). "Ivan Cankar na križpotju romanskih, germanskih in slovanskih literatur." *Sodobnost, 30,* 1184–1188.

Kos, J. (1983). "K vprašanju zvrsti v slovenski pripovedni prozi." *Primerjalna književnost, 6,* 1–16.

Kos, J. (1984). "Evropski vplivi v romanopisju slovenske moderne." *Slavistična revija, 32,* 75–92.

Kos, J. (1984). "Znanost in vera kot kulturni problem." *Sodobnost, 32* (10), 919–942.

Kos, J. (1984). "Znanost in vera kot kulturni problem." *Sodobnost, 32* (12), 1095–1113.

Kos, J. (1987). *Primerjalna zgodovina slovenske literature.* Ljubljana: Znanstveni inštitut filozofske fakultete, Partizanska knjiga.

Kos, J. (1996). "Cankarjeva razmerja do krščanstva, revolucije, spolnosti." *Nova revija, 15* (Ampak), 13–17.

Krashen, S. D. (1982). "Accounting for child-adult differences in second language rate and attainment." In Krashen, S. D., M. H. Long, & R. C. Scarcella (Eds.), *Child-adult differences in second language acquisition* (pp. 202–226). Rowley, MA: Newbury House.

Krashen, S. D., M. H. Long, & R. C. Scarcella (1979). "Age, rate, and eventual attainment in second language acquisition). *TESOL Quarterly, 13,* 579–582.

Krashen, Stephen D. (1981). *Second Language Acquisition and Second Language Learning.* Oxford, New York, Toronto, Sydney, Frankfurt: Pergamon Press.

Krashen, Stephen D. (1982). *Principles and Practice in Second Language Acquisition.* Oxford, New York, Toronto, Sydney, Frankfurt: Pergamon Press.

Kreft, B. (1969). "Cankar in ruska književnost." *Slavistična revija, 17,* 69–98.

Kristan, A. (A. Goršič) (1918). "Nove slovenske knjige." *Naprej, 28* (Junij), 1.

Lah, I. (1918). "Nova Cankarjeva knjiga." *Književni jug, 1* (1. April), 271–277.

Lefevere, A. (1982). "Translated Literature in the Study of Literature." In *Translation in the Literary Process* (pp. 41–62). Nitra: Nitrianske tlačiarne.

Lefevere, A. (1990). "Translation: Its Genealogy in the West." In A. Lefevere & S. Bassnett (Eds.), *Translation, History and Culture* (pp. 14–28). London, New York: Pinter.

Lefevere, A. (1992). *Translation, History, Culture: A Sourcebook.* London, New York: Routledge.

Lefevere, A. (1995a). "Chinese and Western Thinking on Translation". Unpublished lecture at "Cetra translation seminar" in Leuven, 1–31.

Lefevere, A. (1995b). "Is this the same text?: A Consumer's Approach to Translation". Unpublished lecture at "Cetra translation seminar" in Leuven, 1–31.

Lefevere, A. (1990). In Susan Bassnett (Eds.), *Translation: History and Culture.* London: Pinter.

Leksikon pisaca Jugoslavije I (A-Dž) (1972. S.v). "Cankar, Ivan." Beograd: Matica srpska.

Littlewood, W. (1984). *Foreign and Second Language Learning.* Cambridge: Cambridge University Press.

Long, Michael H. (1990). Maturational Constraints on Language Development. *Studies in Second Language Acquisition, 12,* 251–285.

Luther, M. (1963). "Sendbrief vom Dolmetschen." In Hans Joachim Störig (Ed.), *Das Problem des Übersetzens* (pp. 18–22). Darmstadt: Wiessenschaftliche Buchgesellschaft.

Mahnič, J. (1956/57). "Slog in ritem Cankarjeve proze." *Jezik in slovstvo, 2,* 97–104, 152–159, 208–217.

Mahnič, J. (1964). *Zgodovina slovenskega slovstva* V. Ljubljana: Slovenska matica.
Mahnič, J. (1969). "Značilnosti slovenske moderne." *V. seminar slovenskega jezika, literature in kulture.* Ljubljana: Univerza v Ljubljani, Filozofska fakulteta, Oddelek za slovanske jezike in književnosti.
Man, Paul de (1991). "Conclusions: La Tache du Traducteur de Walter Benjamin." *Traduire la théorie TTR, IV* (2), 21–52.
Mazovec, I. (1917). "Kultura." *Jugoslovan* (29 December), 3.
McAlester, G. (1992). "Teaching Translation into a Foreign Language: Status, Scope and Aims." In C. Dollerup & A. Loddegaard (Eds.), *Teaching Translation and Interpreting: Training, Talent and Experience* (pp. 291–297). Amsterdam, Philadelphia: John Benjamins.
Medgyes, P. (1994). *The Non-Native Teacher.* Hong Kong: MacMillan Publishers.
Mehrez, S. (1992). "Translation and the Postcolonial Experience: The Francophone North African Text." In Lawrence Venuti (Ed.), *Rethinking Translation: Discourse, Subjectivity, Ideology.* New York, London: Routledge.
Merhar, I. (1904). "Ivan Cankar: *Hiša Marije Pomočnice.*" *Ljubljanski zvon,* 24, 379–380, 435–436.
Močnik, R. (1971). "Meščevo zlato." *Problemi,* 9 (106/107), 44–88.
Moder, J. (1985). *Slovenski leksikon novejšega prevajanja.* Koper: Založba lipa.
Neubert, A., & Gregory M. Shreve (1992). *Translation as Text.* Kent, Ohio and London: The Kent State University Press.
Newmark, P. (1981). *Approaches to Translation.* Oxford, New York, Toronto, Sydney, Frankfurt: Pergamon Press.
Newport, E. L. (1990). "Maturational Constraints on Language Learning." *Cognitive Science,* 14 (1), 11–28.
Nida, E. (1964). *Toward a Science of Translating: With Special Reference to Principles and Procedures Involved in Bible Translating.* Leiden: E. J. Brill.
Nida, E., & Taber C. R. (1982). *The Theory and Practice of Translation.* Leiden: The United Bible Society, E. J. Brill.
Ozvald, K. (1920). "Cankar zagovornik ponižanih in razžaljenih." *Dom in svet,* 33, 45–47.
Paikeday, T. M. (1985). *The Native Speaker is Dead!: An informal discussion of a linguistic myth with Noam Chomsky and other linguists, philosophers, psychologists, and lexicographers.* Toronto, New York: Paikeday Publishing Inc.
Petrič, J. (1978). "Adamičevo prevajanje slovenskih umetnostnih del v angleščino." *Slavistična revija,* 26, 417–441.
Petrič, J. (1978). "Louis Adamic as an interpreter of Yugoslav literature in America." *Acta neophilologica,* 11, 29–46.
Petrič, J. (1981). "Louis Adamič and his views concerning literature." *Slovenski koledar '82,* 29 (October), 285–288.
Petrič, J. (1989). "Louisa Adamiča prevajanje v angleščino." In Frane Jerman et al. (Eds.), *Radovljiški prevajalski zbornik.* Ljubljana: DSKP.
Phillipson, R. (1992). *Linguistic Imperialism.* Oxford: Oxford University Press.
Pinker, S. (1994). *The Language Instinct: The New Science of Language and Mind.* London, New York, Ringwood, Toronto, Aukland: Penguin Group.
Pirjevec, D. (1964). *Ivan Cankar in evropska literatura.* Ljubljana: Cankarjeva založba.

Pogorelec, B. (1969). "Zgradba stavka v prozi Ivana Cankarja." *V. seminar slovenskega jezika, literature in kulture.* Ljubljana: Univerza v Ljubljani, Filozofska fakulteta, Oddelek za slovanske jezike in književnosti.

Pogorelec, B. (1976). "Ivan Cankar – vozlišče razvoja slovenske besedne umetnosti." *XII. seminar slovenskega jezika, literature in kulture* (pp. 27–45). Ljubljana: Univerza v Ljubljani, Filozofska fakulteta, Oddelek za slovanske jezike in književnosti.

Pogorelec, B. (1976/77). "Cankarjevo izročilo." *Jezik in slovstvo, 22,* 240–247.

Pogorelec, B. (1976/77). "Ivan Cankar – Vozlišče slovenskega slovstvenega razvoja." *Jezik in slovstvo, 22,* 129–135.

Pogorelec, B. (1977). "O dveh značilnostih Cankarjevega sloga: Gramatična figura in metafora." In J. Vidmar, Š. Barbarič, & F. Zadravec (Eds.), *Simpozij o Ivanu Cankarju 1976.* Ljubljana: Slovenska matica.

Pregelj, I. (1917/18). "Literaren uvod v *Podobe iz sanj." Mentor, 5* (6), 78–85.

Pym, A. (1998). "Spanish tradition." In Mona Baker (Ed.), *Routledge Encyclopedia of Translation Studies* (pp. 552–560). London, New York: Routledge.

Quirk, R. (1990). "Language Varieties and Standard Language." *English Today, 21* (6/1), 3–10.

Rajagopalan, Kanavillil (1999). "Of EFL teachers, conscience, and cowardice." *ELT Journal, 53* (3 July), 200–206.

Rampton, M. B. H. (1990). "Displacing the 'native speaker': Expertise, Affiliation, and Inheritance." *ELT Journal, 44* (2), 97–101.

Robinson, D. (1997). *Western Translation Theory: From Herodotus to Nietzsche.* Manchester: St. Jerome Publishing.

Ross, J. R. (1979). "Where is English?" In Fillmore, C. J., D. Kempler, & W. S.-Y. Wang (Eds.), *Individual Differences in Language Ability and Language Behavior* (pp. 127–163). New York: Academic Press.

Samuelsson-Brown, G. (1995). *A Practical Guide for Translators.* Clevedon, Philadelphia, Adelaide: Multilingual Matters.

Schleiermacher, F. (1985). "Über die verschiedenen Methoden des Übersetzens". In *Les Tours de Babel: essais sur la traduction.* Mauvezin: Editions Trans-Europ-Repress, 279–347.

Simon, S. (1996). *Gender in Translation: Cultural Identity and the Politics of Transmission.* London, New York: Routledge.

Singleton, D. (1992). "Second Language Instruction: The When and How". In Language Teaching in the Twenty-first Century: Problems and Prospects. *AILA Review, 9,* 46–54.

Singleton, David (2001). "Age and Second Language Acquisition." *Annual Review of Applied Linguistics, 21,* 77–89.

Skutnabb-Kangas, T., & Phillipson, R. (1989). " 'Mother Tongue': The Theoretical and Sociopolitical Construction of a Concept." In Ulrich Ammon (Ed.), *Status and Function of Languages and Language Varieties* (pp. 450–477). Berlin, New York: Walter Gruyter.

Slodnjak, A. (1969). "Ivan Cankar: *Hiša Marije Pomočnice." Slavistična revija, 17,* 183–191.

Slodnjak, A. (1976). "Introduction." In Ivan Cankar, *The Ward of Our Lady of Mercy.* Ljubljana: Državna založba Slovenije.

Slodnjak, A. (1981). "Ivan Cankar in Slovene and World Literature." *The Slavonic and East European Review, 59* (2), 186–196.

Slovar slovenskega književnega jezika I–V. (1970–1991). Edited by Slovenska akademija znanosti in umetnosti, Znanstvenoraziskovalni center Slovenske akademije znanosti in umetnosti, Inštitut za slovenski jezika Frana Ramovša. Ljubljana: Državna založba Slovenije.

Snell-Hornby, M. (1992). "The Professional Translator of Tomorrow: Language Specialist or All-round Expert?." In C. Dollerup & A. Loddegaard (Eds.), *Teaching Translation and Interpreting: Training, Talent and Experience* (pp. 9–22). Amsterdam, Philadelphia: John Benjamins.

Snell-Hornby, M. (1995. [1988]). *Translation Studies: An Integrated Approach*. Amsterdam, Philadelphia: John Benjamins.

Sokačić, Ž. (1918). "Misli o Cankaru povodom njegove knjige *Podobe iz sanj*." *Savremenik, 9*, 428–430.

Sovre, A. (1956/57). "Daktiloidnost Cankarjeve proze." *Jezik in slovstvo, 2*, 326–327.

Steiner, G. (1992 [1975]). *After Babel: Aspects of Language and Translation*. New York, Oxford: Oxford University Press.

Stern, H. H. (1983). *Fundamental Concepts of Language Teaching*. Oxford: Oxford University Press.

Stolze, R. (1994). *Übersetzungstheorien: Eine Einfuhrung*. Tübingen: Gunter Narr Verlag.

Susel, Rudolf M. (1992). "Poslanstvo in vloga časopisa *Ameriška domovina*." *Dve domovini, 2* (3), 237–251.

Toury, G. (1980). *In Search of a Theory of Translation*. Tel Aviv: The Porter Institute for Poetics and Semiotics.

Toury, G. (1985). "A Rationale for Descriptive Translation Studies." In T. Hermans (Ed.), *The Manipulation of Literature: Studies in Literary Translation*. London, Sydney: Croom Helm.

Toury, G. (1995). *Descriptive Translation Studies and Beyond*. Amsterdam: John Benjamins.

Venuti, L. (1995). *The Translator's Invisibility: A History of Translation*. London, New York: Routledge.

Venuti, L. (1998). *The Scandals of Translation: Towards an Ethics of Difference*. London, New York: Routledge.

Venuti, L. (2000). "Translation, Community, Utopia." In Lawrence Venuti (Ed.), *The Translation Studies Reader* (pp. 468–488). London, New York: Routledge.

Verč, I. (1977). "Cankar in Dostojevski: nastavitev nekaterih problemov. Simpozij o Ivanu Cankarju na tržaški univerzi." *Sodobnost, 25*, 754–758.

Vidmar, J. (1971). "Ivan Cankar." Introdution to Ivan Cankar. *My Life and other Sketches* (pp. 7–13). Ljubljana: Državna založba Slovenije.

Vidmar, J. (1977). "Tri Cankarjeve orientacije. In J. Vidmar, Š. Barbarič, & F. Zadravec (Eds.), *Simpozij o Ivanu Cankarju 1976*. Ljubljana: Slovenska matica.

Vodnik, F. (1935). " 'Propad' Ivana Cankarja." *Dom in svet, 48*, 110–112.

Vodnik, F. (1935). "Ivan Cankar: Zbrani spisi." *Dom in svet, 48*, 444–447.

Yule, G. (1985). *The Study of Language: An Introduction*. Cambridge: Cambridge University Press.

Zadravec, F. (1976). "Subjektivne in objektivne osnove Cankarjeve satire." *Slavistična revija, 24*, 57–70.

Zadravec, F. (1982). "Ivan Cankar kot naturalist in realist v teoriji in praksi." *Obdobje realizma v slovenskem jeziku, književnosti in kulturi* (pp. 73–100). Ljubljana: Univerza v Ljubljani, Filozofska fakulteta, Oddelek za slovanske jezike in književnosti.

Zadravec, F. (1989). "Odtisi Dostojevskega v slovenski poetiški, filozofski in estetiški zavesti v prvi polovici XX. stoletja." *Slavistična revija, 37,* 403–427.

Zadravec, F. (1991). *Cankarjeva ironija.* Murska Sobota: Pomurska založba in Ljubljana: Znanstveni inštitut filozofske fakultete.

Žižek, S. (1978). "Dva aspekta." *Problemi, 16* (177–180), 205–209.

Žorž, B. (1989). "*Hlapec Jernej in njegova pravica*: Poskus sodobne psihološke interpretacije." *Primorska srečanja, 13* (97), 418–420.

Index

In the series *Benjamins Translation Library* the following titles have been published thus far or are scheduled for publication:

37 **TIRKKONEN-CONDIT, Sonja and Riitta JÄÄSKELÄINEN (eds.):** Tapping and Mapping the Processes of Translation and Interpreting. Outlooks on empirical research. 2000. x, 176 pp.

38 **SCHÄFFNER, Christina and Beverly ADAB (eds.):** Developing Translation Competence. 2000. xvi, 244 pp.

39 **CHESTERMAN, Andrew, Natividad GALLARDO SAN SALVADOR and Yves GAMBIER (eds.):** Translation in Context. Selected papers from the EST Congress, Granada 1998. 2000. x, 393 pp.

40 **ENGLUND DIMITROVA, Birgitta and Kenneth HYLTENSTAM (eds.):** Language Processing and Simultaneous Interpreting. Interdisciplinary perspectives. 2000. xvi, 164 pp.

41 **NIDA, Eugene A.:** Contexts in Translating. 2002. x, 127 pp.

42 **HUNG, Eva (ed.):** Teaching Translation and Interpreting 4. Building bridges. 2002. xii, 243 pp.

43 **GARZONE, Giuliana and Maurizio VIEZZI (eds.):** Interpreting in the 21st Century. Challenges and opportunities. 2002. x, 337 pp.

44 **SINGERMAN, Robert:** Jewish Translation History. A bibliography of bibliographies and studies. With an introductory essay by Gideon Toury. 2002. xxxvi, 420 pp.

45 **ALVES, Fabio (ed.):** Triangulating Translation. Perspectives in process oriented research. 2003. x, 165 pp.

46 **BRUNETTE, Louise, Georges BASTIN, Isabelle HEMLIN and Heather CLARKE (eds.):** The Critical Link 3. Interpreters in the Community. Selected papers from the Third International Conference on Interpreting in Legal, Health and Social Service Settings, Montréal, Quebec, Canada 22–26 May 2001. 2003. xii, 359 pp.

47 **SAWYER, David B.:** Fundamental Aspects of Interpreter Education. Curriculum and Assessment. 2004. xviii, 312 pp.

48 **MAURANEN, Anna and Pekka KUJAMÄKI (eds.):** Translation Universals. Do they exist? 2004. vi, 224 pp.

49 **PYM, Anthony:** The Moving Text. Localization, translation, and distribution. 2004. xviii, 223 pp.

50 **HANSEN, Gyde, Kirsten MALMKJÆR and Daniel GILE (eds.):** Claims, Changes and Challenges in Translation Studies. Selected contributions from the EST Congress, Copenhagen 2001. 2004. xiv, 320 pp. **[EST Subseries 1]**

51 **CHAN, Leo Tak-hung:** Twentieth-Century Chinese Translation Theory. Modes, issues and debates. 2004. xvi, 277 pp.

52 **HALE, Sandra Beatriz:** The Discourse of Court Interpreting. Discourse practices of the law, the witness and the interpreter. 2004. xviii, 267 pp.

53 **DIRIKER, Ebru:** De-/Re-Contextualizing Conference Interpreting. Interpreters in the Ivory Tower? 2004. x, 223 pp.

54 **GONZÁLEZ DAVIES, Maria:** Multiple Voices in the Translation Classroom. Activities, tasks and projects. 2004. x, 262 pp.

55 **ANGELELLI, Claudia V.:** Revisiting the Interpreter's Role. A study of conference, court, and medical interpreters in Canada, Mexico, and the United States. 2004. xvi, 127 pp.

56 **ORERO, Pilar (ed.):** Topics in Audiovisual Translation. 2004. xiv, 227 pp.

57 **CHERNOV, Ghelly V.:** Inference and Anticipation in Simultaneous Interpreting. A probability-prediction model. Edited with a critical foreword by Robin Setton and Adelina Hild. 2004. xxx, 268 pp. **[EST Subseries 2]**

58 **BRANCHADELL, Albert and Lovell Margaret WEST (eds.):** Less Translated Languages. 2005. viii, 416 pp.

59 **MALMKJÆR, Kirsten (ed.):** Translation in Undergraduate Degree Programmes. 2004. vi, 202 pp.

60 **TENNENT, Martha (ed.):** Training for the New Millennium. Pedagogies for translation and interpreting. 2005. xxvi, 276 pp.

61 **HUNG, Eva (ed.):** Translation and Cultural Change. Studies in history, norms and image-projection. xvi, 188 pp. + index. *Expected June 2005*

62 **POKORN, Nike K.:** Challenging the Traditional Axioms. Translation into a non-mother tongue. 2005. xii, 163 pp. **[EST Subseries 3]**

63 **JANZEN, Terry (ed.):** Topics in Signed Language Interpreting. Theory and practice. *Expected October 2005*

A complete list of titles in this series can be found on **www.benjamins.com/jbp**